Making Music and Memories from
Country to Jazz, Blues to Rock

THIS OLD
Guitar

With stories and photographs by Charles Shaar Murray, Dan Forte,
Teisco Del Rey, Michael Wright, Douglas B. Green, Tommy Womack,
Ward Meeker, *Vintage Guitar* magazine, and more.

Voyageur Press
A Town Square Book

Text copyright © 2003 by Voyageur Press, Inc.
Photographs and artwork copyright © 2003 by photographers and artists as noted

Edited by Margret Aldrich and Michael Dregni
Designed by JoDee Mittlestadt
Printed in China

03   04   05   06   07   5   4   3   2   1

Library of Congress Cataloging-in-Publication Data available

ISBN 0-89658-631-6

Distributed in Canada by Raincoast Books,
9050 Shaughnessy Street, Vancouver, B.C. V6P 6E5

Published by Voyageur Press, Inc.
123 North Second Street, P.O. Box 338,
Stillwater, MN 55082 U.S.A.
651-430-2210, fax 651-430-2211
books@voyageurpress.com
www.voyageurpress.com

Educators, fundraisers, premium and gift buyers, publicists, and marketing managers: Looking for creative products and new sales ideas? Voyageur Press books are available at special discounts when purchased in quantities, and special editions can be created to your specifications. For details contact the marketing department at 800-888-9653.

Legal Notice
This is not an official publication of Fender, Gibson, Gretsch, National, Rickenbacker, Bear Creek, or any other guitar manufacturer. Certain names, model designations, and logo designs are the property of trademark holders. We use them for identification purposes only. Neither the editor, photographer, publisher, nor this book are in any way affiliated with Fender, Gibson, Gretsch, National, Rickenbacker, Bear Creek, or any other guitar manufacturer.

Permissions
    "Music, Sweet Music, Drips From My Fender's Fingers: Hendrix and Hardware" by Charles Shaar Murray from *Crosstown Traffic*. Copyright © 1989 by Charles Shaar Murray. Reprinted by permission of St. Martin's Press.
    "In the Beginning There Was Revelation" by Tommy Womack from *Cheese Chronicles*. Copyright © 1995 by Eggman Publishing. Reprinted by permission of Tommy Womack.

On the frontispiece: Duded up in full Hopalong Cassidy gear, Junior poses with his guitar. A Hawaiian miss strums her uke. A 1950s Gibson Les Paul Standard Duo. (Photograph © *Vintage Guitar*)

On the title pages: A trio of Bear Creek Weissenborn-style Hollowneck Hawaiian guitars built by luthier Bill Hardin. From left, Bear Creek's Hollowneck MK Edition, Artists/Collector's Edition, and Kona model with German spruce top. (Courtesy Bill and B. J. Hardin/Bear Creek Guitars)

Opposite page: Cowgirl Patsy Montana sings around the campfire.

Opposite the contents page: A custom red pre-CBS Fender Telecaster. Owner: Craig Brody. (Photograph © *Vintage Guitar*)

Acknowledgments

Many people helped shape this book and string together the stories, memories, and tall tales collected here. Our sincere thanks to Sigrid Arnott; Eric Dregni; Michelle Filkins; Dan Forte and Teisco Del Rey; Ranger Douglas B. Green; Mikki Halpin; B. J. and Bill Hardin of Bear Creek Guitars; Gary Kunkel; Leif Larsen; Dennis McGregor; Ward Meeker and *Vintage Guitar* magazine; Karl Hagstrom Miller; Dorthy Molstad and Dennis Fleischauer; Charles Shaar Murray; Scott Puckett; Tommy Womack; and Michael Wright.

Contents

Home—Be It Ever So Humble
Just a Song at Twilight

THIS OLD
Guitar

My first guitar was a Made-in-China special purchased at a Salvation Army store for the astronomical sum of twelve dollars. I remember it as though it was yesterday: That guitar seemed to have an inner glow, speaking just to me in clichés from amongst the rusting Roy Rogers lunchboxes, formerly chic foam-injected conquistador artwork, and swooned-out Bobby Sherman LPs. Twelve bucks was a lot for a twelve-year-old punk kid in those buzz-cut days of summers past. I had to abstain from baseball cards for weeks to afford it—and even then my ma anteed up six dollars in a kind-hearted donation her ears probably came to regret many times over.

My guitar was a typical plastic-string classical with a plywood fretboard stained dark to fake rosewood, a solid top that suffered abominable abuses (see below), and plywood sides that probably came straight from a 1960s paneled basement. Yet the guitar body seemed to actually resonate, at least to my untutored ear, and a glorious tone emitted from that fake-rosette soundhole. I was now suddenly, instantly, unimpeachably cool.

The inspiration in buying the guitar was that same hormone that seems to kick in for boys and girls at about age twelve—an unnamed, unstudied, but obviously widely distributed chemical reaction that drives youth to get a guitar and make loud noises out in the garage. The guitar is without doubt *the* musical instrument that played the soundtrack to the twentieth century, and playing bad guitar in a bad band has become an all-American rite of passage.

I was no different than most kids with their first guitar. I couldn't tune it to save my life—in fact it was years before my fellow bandmates and I even realized we were

THIS OLD GUITAR
The family gathers around on the porch to harmonize as the sun sets in the west.

supposed to tune our instrument to *each other* let alone some set low E cycle that someone somewhere had ordained as the great "in tune" truth. It took me weeks of finger contortions following the arcane diagrams in a Mel Bay book to form my first C chord. This was digital gymnastics that made my fingers ache, and it was months before I could strum a three-chord song without an intermission between chords long enough to get more popcorn. Holding a pick in my right hand was something I still haven't mastered: Those darn celluloid Model 351s always wanted to get loose, just like my pet white mouse, which finally disappeared down the heating duct. And then there was the issue of playing in time, an issue that remains an issue to this day.

But miracles do happen. After several months, I could finger the theme to The Ventures' "Wipe Out" as if I surfed the big ones every day after I got home from sixth grade. And I was strumming those C chords like a pro, although the Em chord, which only required two fingers side by side on the same fret, remained my fave.

Problem was, my classical guitar simply didn't rock.

This is a dilemma most kids suffer through at this stage. Happily, the solution is simple: You put stickers on your guitar. Back in the 1960s, the key was an STP sticker in some sort of near-fanatical devotion us kids must have had to oil additives. My guitar suddenly sounded better, but it didn't yet twang.

The solution here was of course to throw away those plastic strings and run steel strings on my classical guitar. Suddenly, twang was mine—at the expense of my classical guitar's top, which slowly caved in, and the bridge, which needed a couple good long wood screws to hold it rock steady.

Now I had the stickers and the twang but I was still lacking that Holy Grail: volume. For an acoustic guitar, there's only one thing to do: amplification. I again curbed my baseball card habit as well as my root

1960s FENDER CUSTOM COLOR DUO
1962 lefthanded Olympic White Fender Stratocaster and 1963 Purple Sparkle Telecaster. Owner: Craig Brody. (Photograph © *Vintage Guitar*)

beer love in the bargain and saved up to buy a pickup. This bolted nicely to the guitar's top and I plugged the cord into the back of my parents' stereo when they weren't looking. There's no better feeling for a youthful rebel with a guitar than that moment when you Go Electric, feel the power unleashed in your hands, and understand that universal guitar truth: Loudness is next to godliness.

Everything now progressed in a blur. I figured out the signature lick (all by myself!) to The Rolling Stones' "(I Can't Get No) Satisfaction." I learned my first barre chord and worked on my all-important musical coordination so I could jump off my bed in time to the windmill power strum. I even began writing a song about some cute girl in my sixth-grade class, a song that to my everlasting good fortune was never sung. The future looked bright: With a bit more practice, I might even be able to pick out "Smoke on the Water" with my teeth or "Proud Mary" with my guitar behind my head!

Yet my Frankenstein's monster of a guitar was still not quite right. True, it was lacking the all-important whammy bar, but with a little pressure on that poor, overstressed soundboard I could get the strings to bend in a cool vibrato. And yes, I only had one pickup with little tone control through my parents' rapidly deteriorating stereo, but those overworked speakers had developed some cool distortion. My guitar just didn't look the part (even with the STP sticker). I needed a solid-body with cutaways and curves. More knobs! More buttons! A toggle switch!

I hatched a plan to saw the neck off my classical guitar and bolt it onto a budget body bought separately, but while I had proven my strength with a screwdriver, my electrical skills—required for soldering in pickups and tone-pots—ended with changing a record on the stereo. So it was back to mowing grass and shoveling snow to save my pennies for a solid-body.

It took some time, but I eventually bought a secondhand, bare-bones Fender Esquire—a guitar that was in those days just "used," long before anyone was talking "pre-CBS," "vintage," or even cared if it was all original. With that v-necked, cream-colored Esquire came a little, homely tweed-covered Fender amp that sounded even better than the tone-torn speakers in our

HAWAIIAN JAM
Elvis jams with the islanders in *Blue Hawaii*.

stereo (if that was possible!) and could be rolled all the way up to a gut-rousing "10."

Fame and fortune didn't come with that guitar, but at a certain point in life you don't expect that anymore. Our garage band parted amicably—and mercifully. None of us became musicians because none of us were musicians in the first place. But we all still keep in touch, and if they're anything like me, they too still noodle around on their guitars and basses and drums when the day is done.

This story isn't anything special. In fact, it's a simple coming-of-age tale lived out by boys and girls everywhere. For most of us, time can be divided into the years before we got our first guitar and after.

Many of the stories, tall tales, essays, and reminiscences in this anthology tell of that first guitar in one way or another. The authors include some famous guitar historians and journalists, a university professor who practices what he teaches, one woman suffering Post-Traumatic Guitar Boredom Syndrome, and even several actual musicians. All have a good yarn to share.

Much of the photography comes from the good graces and archives of *Vintage Guitar* magazine. Many of the historical images were found in folks' scrapbooks and photo albums.

If you still remember that first guitar, still play guitar, still turn your amp to "10," or still dream guitars, then this book is for you. Enjoy!

First Love

FIRST LOVE
Love blossoms on the beach with just a guitar and thou.

Field of Dreams

By Michael Wright

Michael Wright knows his guitars. Since learning to play the ukulele in 1952, the professional writer, historian, musician, and guitar collector has gone on to pen several books and acquire six hundred guitars. The co-author of such tomes as Classic Guitars of the Fifties *and* Electric Guitars: The Illustrated Encyclopedia *has also served as host for the radio show "Guitaromania" and acted as a consultant to Boston's Museum of Fine Arts guitar design exhibit, "Dangerous Curves," which included a generous sampling from his impressive collection. This essay records Michael's initiation into the realm of guitars, bringing to light what first persuaded him to pick up a six-string and what still inspires him today.*

 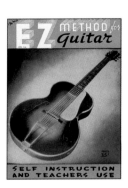 

Blame it on Johnny Unitas. Not because I didn't make it to the NFL. No, you could say it's his fault that I chose the ringing jangle of a *guitar* as my playing field for drawing attention to myself.

As with so many of us, it all goes back to that time when the hormones started kicking in and the accompanying need to find an identity that I imagined would be attractive to the fairer sex. For me, it was 1959 and the world was full of possibilities in our comfortable little Michigan town. What could I become?

Actually, the first hint that everything *wasn't* possible can be laid at Al Kaline's feet. Kaline was the immensely talented outfielder for the Detroit Tigers, whose games we followed on our colorful Made-In-Japan, pocket transistor radios. Boy, I was gonna be a star just like him. Until I tried out for the Little League team that spring. Oh, I hit the ball ok, but no home runs and, well, when the grounders started rolling past my glove through my legs, I reluctantly relinquished that pathway.

ANGEL WITH A UKULELE
A youngster is transported into a heavenly state as he picks his uke.

Summer went by with no field of dreams. Then it was time for football tryouts. On my neighborhood corner lot I could pull the entire other team into the end zone. I could be like the Baltimore Colts' Unitas, whose last-minute, game-winning passes to Ray Berry fueled my fantasies courtesy of the weekend radio network airwaves. I didn't even make the first cut. Clearly I was in need of a different angle.

That's when I realized that there might be a more *unconventional* route to achieving my goal: the guitar. After all, what is performing but getting attention? I'd learned to play years earlier on the proverbial guitar with 3/4" action, but we'd moved and I'd drifted away from it. I loved hearing Mr. Chet play, and my favorite commercial was for Robert Hall's (where we bought my Sunday suit once a year), performed by Les Paul and Mary Ford. Maybe a guitar could catch ladies' eyes. Besides, that was the scam Dobie Gillis was always working on TV at the time, hanging out at the coffee house with Maynard G. Krebbs and trying to learn how to play guitar to get chicks (even though all he got was Zelda). That could be my ticket.

Moving into the '60s was a good time to be into guitar. You heard them everywhere. Ricky Nelson (and

BORN TO ROCK
Some folk play with teddy bears, some with super heroes. Others were born to rock.

James Burton) on *Ozzie & Harriet*. The theme song to *Bonanza*. Hank Garland's solo on Marty Robbins' "El Paso." The boogie track to Johnny Bond's "Hot Rod Lincoln." My god, the Ventures' "Walk, Don't Run" and Jorgan Ingmann's "Apache!" And folk music was just beginning to break big. I applied myself and before long I didn't feel right without six strings under my fingers.

My first gig was in church playing gospel tunes on a Harmony-made guitar I'd bought from a mail-order catalog using money I'd earned from a paper route. In subsequent years I progressed from Gospel to folk, rock, and classical guitar playing. My favorite performance trick was to build with familiar tunes and then pull out a surprise, something unusual, unexpected. I'm sure my guitar playing drew the attention of a few girls, but it never led to romance . . . or even, alas, any groupies. Not even a Zelda. But it did give me the identity I'd wanted, one that's sustained me for the rest of my life.

During my musical peregrinations, I discovered that the guitar itself could become an effective tool of attraction. And true to the epiphany that drove me into the arms of the guitar, I found myself increasingly attracted to unconventional guitars. The seeds were no doubt already there. In college, when everyone was slavering over Martin guitars, I defended my Harmony, until I got enough bread together from teaching to purchase a less fashionable Guild. When others were playing a Ramirez, I was playing a guitar by a then little known maker Robert Ruck. But the strongest affection for strange came in the realm of electric guitars, which, after all, represent the greatest opportunity for the obscure, unusual, and wonderful.

This first manifested itself when, after many years of only owning a classical guitar, I decided to buy an electric guitar. Did I even think of buying a Fender Stratocaster? No, I went straight to a pawnshop and found a late '60s four-pickup Kent in gorgeous birdseye maple. Four pickups. They're better than three, aren't they?

I'll never forget the night I was in a hole-in-the-wall used guitar shop in Southwest Philly. We were shooting the breeze when in walked a guy who had two guitars he wanted to sell, including a Gibson Les Paul. The owners swooped down on the Les Paul and started oohing and aahing over this nice but conventional and fairly plain instrument. But it was when they casually opened the other case to see what was there that my jaw dropped. It was a dead mint 1982 Electra Endorser, a kind of Japanese Les Paul with a different shape and heelless neck, fancy inlays and lots of binding, what turned out to be killer hot pickups, *and* a quilted maple top that's a psychedelic trip to stare into. I offered them three bucks to take it off their hands immediately and they waved their hands and went back to admiring the Les Paul. Which of us was crazier?

It got better . . . or worse. Rather than the influence of an athletic idol, this was inspired by that pretty little Kent guitar. I began to peer into back racks of music stores and pawnshops, at the stuff collecting dust. Not looking for Les Pauls and Stratocasters, but *copies* of those guitars, with amusing names like Love Rock and a spaghetti-logo Tokai. Then came '60s Japanese Teiscos with built-in amps that even work sometimes. A whacky blue Wandré guitar with an outside-the-body aluminum neck and linoleum trim. A gold-stenciled KayKraft Venetian acoustic archtop from the 1930s with a bolt-on neck sporting a weird, concave neck adjustment device. An obscure Player guitar with pickup modules you can remove and replace from the back while you're playing! Trawling through trading newspapers. Wheedling down the price on a rare headless one-piece Modulus Graphite Monocoque. Time went by and the obsession with—and quantity of—unusual guitars grew.

1964 GIBSON FIREBIRD V
Detail of the Vibrola on a Cardinal Red Firebird V. Owner: Brian Fischer. (Photograph © *Vintage Guitar*)

1920s MARTIN LINEUP

Above: C. F. Martin & Co.'s guitars made a name for themselves due not to their no-frills style but for their solid construction and glorious tone. The smallest of Martin's O Series harken back to the era of parlor guitars whereas the larger OM Series were more modern in look, sound, and volume. From left, a 1923 O-21; 1927 OO-45; and 1923 OM-28. Owners: From left, Buddy Summer; Nancy's Music Box; Steve Sassano. (Photograph © *Vintage Guitar*)

1954 FENDER STRATOCASTER

Opposite page: Upon its debut in 1954, the Stratocaster was the most outlandish Space Age guitar imaginable. It was also the dream come true for many musicians as well as youngsters drooling as they gazed into music-store windows. The guitar's solid body and inexpensive assembly-line production were still being scoffed at over at Gibson, but the Strat boasted classy curved body contours, a lineup of three pickups, a radical "Tremolo System" bridge with separate string trees, and controls that were easy to use, efficient, and offered numerous possibilities for experimentation. Others might have laughed, but the Strat soon became the most popular guitar—ever. Owner: Thoroughbred Music. (Photograph © *Vintage Guitar*)

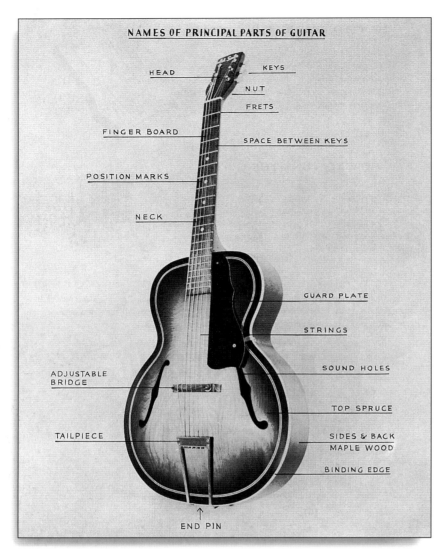

NAMES OF PRINCIPAL PARTS OF GUITAR

HEAD

KEYS

NUT

FRETS

FINGER BOARD

SPACE BETWEEN KEYS

POSITION MARKS

NECK

GUARD PLATE

STRINGS

SOUND HOLES

ADJUSTABLE BRIDGE

TOP SPRUCE

TAILPIECE

SIDES & BACK MAPLE WOOD

BINDING EDGE

END PIN

GUITAR ANATOMY 101

BARNYARD ROCK
Opposite page: Sis jams on her new guitar.

The guitars became as much the attraction as the music. The surprise became the instrument to be played next. Sparkle is fun for the player but subtle for the audience. Goofy technology—like a Ripley Stereo's individual string output (or four pickups, for that matter!)—is great for the player, but invisible to the average mother-my-dog audience. Weird shapes— like a moon-shaped Kawai Moonsault or Kramer Triaxe spacecruiser—are much better crowd-pleasers. Great colors can't be beat . . . though there's differences of opinion about the manliness of my *hot pink* Peavey Vandenberg. And sending the crowd "Rollin' and

Tumblin'" with a Guyatone lap steel mounted on legs and shoved through a Rat distortion pedal is sure to bring astonishment and a smile!

Perhaps the best critical judgments in such matters came from the kids, which is as it should be. I began to play "guitar shows" for my son's classes as he went through school. I'm not really sure if he thought this was a positive or a negative, having a parent show off in front of his peers. I'd haul in half a dozen or so guitars, sometimes a mix of acoustics and electrics, sometimes a handful of electrics ranging from traditional to outré. Then, after a rousing medley of "Swamp Thing/Star Spangled Banner," played with plenty of whammy on a Jump-At-Me-Yellow B.C. Rich Eagle with a built-in preamp (for the patriotic part), I'd ask the kids to vote on their favorite guitars. Did ever a Les Paul or Strat win? No. For acoustics, it was always the early '60s shiny chrome-plated, metal-body Gardena Dobro whose surface reflected the rapt faces, hands down. For electrics, it was always close, but always the same: the svelt tapered lines of the seafoam green Ibanez Maxxas that looked so futuristic, the high-tech matte-black all-graphite Bond Electraglide *with* the groovy green, red, and yellow LEDs like some video game controller, and the aforementioned Eagle. Mostly it was that preamp (hands on their ears, grins on their faces) that pushed the Eagle over the top.

Now my son is at that same stage in life where he's got to be thinking about what his identity will be. He's already figured out he won't be the next Alan Iverson. He's not into guitars, yet (except insofar as he can't wait to sell mine when I die). That's all right. It's his turn to choose a path now. I'm just glad I turned out to be so bad at throwing and catching. Give me something out of the ordinary any day! Thank you Johnny U!

BANJOMAN

Junior strums a power chord on his banjo uke.

1960s GIBSON ES-335 TD

Opposite page: The ES-335 was the best of both worlds. Its semi-solid construction curbed at least some feedback yet still gave it the tone of a true hollow body. Previously, guitarists such as jazzman Charlie Christian and blues-stringer T-Bone Walker stuffed rags in their big Gibson archtops to dampen the feedback when they played large halls. Introduced in 1958 and armed with humbuckers from the start, the dot-neck 335s remain some of the best-sounding electric guitars of all time— especially when teamed with a Marshall 50-watt head and amp combo. (Photograph © *Vintage Guitar*)

FIRST GUITARS

"I bought an old piece of guitar from a fella named Frank Hopkins. I gave him a dollar-and-a-half for it. It was nearly all to pieces, but I didn't know the difference. The back was all broken in, but I got it from him and began to play."
—Son House, from the July 1965 interview, "I Can Make My Own Songs," with Julius Lester

"My first guitar was a wooden cigar box for the body and a little tree that I cut off and shaved up to make the neck. I used wooden pegs for the keys, with holes in them to wrap the wires around. I had all of the strings tuned different, but I had to use the same grade wire on all six."
—Albert King

"I started learning to play the guitar when I was 13 on an old Spanish model which my dad picked up for fifty bob. It's funny how little things can change your whole life."
—George Harrison, quoted in Andy Babiuk's *Beatles Gear: All the Fab Four's Instruments, From Stage to Studio*

"I got my first guitar on my birthday in '61, so I was seven, I guess. It had catgut strings and it was a Masonite version of a Roy Rogers guitar. Maybe it was Gene Autry. I know it had a cowboy on it, and it had cows, and rope stencils on it, you know?"
—Stevie Ray Vaughan, from Keri Leigh's *Stevie Ray Vaughan: Soul to Soul*

"My first guitar was an old cigar box I fixed up with nails and strung wire between. I got a few tones like that. Some of the fellows used rubber bands, but this was better because I got to bend the notes, like Mama did [His mother played guitar with Blind Lemon Jefferson]. When I was small, I used to listen to her when I was supposed to be in bed. She'd give me the chills sometimes, so I aimed at getting hold of some of those notes. I was about twelve, I guess, when she loaned me her guitar a time or two. The big day came when [my stepfather] Marco walked me to the store, and I picked out a banjo and paid for it with the change I'd put by."
—T-Bone Walker, from Helen Oakley Dance's *Stormy Monday: The T-Bone Walker Story*

"I started with banjo when I was 15 when my mother taught me some banjo chords."
—John Lennon, from Barry Miles's *John Lennon In His Own Words*

"It was a Stella, a second-handed one. The first time I played on it I made fifty cents at one of those all-night places, and then the man that run it raised me to two-fifty a night, and I knew I was doing right."
—Muddy Waters on his first guitar, from Robert Gordon's *Can't Be Satisfied: The Life and Times of Muddy Waters*

"My father kept his college guitar in the closet. I plunked around on it every once in a while, but I couldn't figure out how to make it work. It didn't make any sense to me. It didn't feel good when I touched it.

"Then, my younger brother Bobby picked up a cowboy-style, arch-top, F-hole guitar at an auction for $1.50 and started playing it. At that time I was interested in R&B. I liked the sound of blues guitar solos, but guitar wasn't the featured instrument on most of the records out then—the saxophone was.

"I waited for records that had guitar solos on them, but they were always too short. I wanted to be able to play my own solos—long ones—so I taught myself how to play the guitar. I didn't bother to learn any chords just blues licks."
—Frank Zappa, *The Real Frank Zappa Book*

"I was living with my grandparents, who raised me, and since I was the only child in the family, they used to spoil me something terrible. So I badgered them until they bought me a plastic Elvis Presley guitar. Of course, it could never stay in tune, but I could put on a Gene Vincent record, look in the mirror and mime.

"When I was fourteen or fifteen, they gave me a real guitar, an acoustic, but it was so hard to play, I actually didn't even try for a while. And pretty soon the neck began to warp. But I did invent chords. I invented E, and I invented A. I thought I had discovered something incredible."
—Eric Clapton, *The Rolling Stone Interviews: The 1980s*

"When I was six years old, Mom and Dad gave me a guitar for my birthday, and Daddy taught me the chords to 'You Are My Sunshine.'"
—Roy Orbison, *The Rolling Stone Interviews: The 1980s*

FIRST GUITAR

It was a brave new world with that first guitar in hand.

"I got my first guitar when I was about nine years old. It took me five years to learn how to tune it. [Laughs] But it was easy from there on."
—The Edge, *The Rolling Stone Interviews: The 1980s*

"On my fifteenth birthday my mother gave me an accordion. I looked at this accordion and I said, 'God, I don't want this accordion. I want an electric guitar.'

"So we took it down to a pawnshop and I got this little Danelectro, an electric guitar with a tiny little amplifier, and man, I was just in heaven."
—Jerry Garcia, *The Rolling Stone Interviews: 1967–1980*

"I went ahead and made me a guitar. I got me a cigar box, I cut me a round hole in the middle of it, take me a little piece of plank, nailed it on to that cigar box, and I got me some screen wire and I made me a bridge back there and raised it up high enough that it would sound inside that little box, and I got me a tune out of it. I kept my tune, and I played from then on. So I got me a guitar of my own when I got to be eight years old."
—Lightnin' Hopkins, from Jas Obrecht's *Rollin' and Tumblin'*

"My first one was a Stella, about two-and-a-half feet long, with the big round hole in it, and it was red, one of their little red guitars. I was making $15 a month, so I paid seven-and-a-half the first month and seven-and-a-half the next one. I kept it for a long, long time."
—B. B. King, from Richard Kostelanetz's *The B. B. King Companion*

"Clarence Richmond, a classmate of mine, became more friendly and loaned me his father's abandoned four-string tenor guitar to learn on. It was my first touch of the strange instrument and it kept me busy exploring the many songs I could pick out on it."
—Chuck Berry, *Chuck Berry: The Autobiography*

"At the age of six, I got my first real guitar. Daddy Nelson put it in my hands. It was a Stella they bought out of a Sears catalogue. The strings were about an inch off the neck. My fingers would bleed from playing it."
—Willie Nelson, *Willie: An Autobiography*

"My father bought me a $25 Stadium-brand guitar for my birthday in October of 1955. He felt that everybody should play a musical instrument and had tried to teach me the piano, but it was no go, so he gave up on me and taught my brother. The guitar was a second attempt on his part."
—Paul Simon

"[I got my first guitar] when I was about 14. It was all a matter of trying to pick up tips and stuff. There weren't many method books, really, apart from jazz which had no bearing on rock and roll whatsoever at that time. But that first guitar was a Grazzioso which was like a copy of a Stratocaster."
—Jimmy Page, *Guitar Player* magazine

"I bought my own first guitar for twenty deutsche marks, about five bucks American at the time, and carried it back to the base with me through the freezing German winter. I'll never forget that walk, four miles through knee-deep snow; I was numb all over. . . .

My guitar survived until 1957, by the way, when my brother Tommy and one of my nephews, horsing around at my house in Memphis, smashed it to pieces by accident and neglected to mention the event until one day when I happened to notice it was missing. I didn't care; by then I had a Martin."
—Johnny Cash, on buying his first guitar while stationed in Germany, *Cash: The Autobiography*

Kramer™

"It's very simply the best guitar you can buy today."
Edward Van Halen

The Evolution of a Gearhead

By Karl Hagstrom Miller

Karl Hagstrom Miller practices what he teaches. A professor of history at the University of Texas at Austin, he has written about music ranging from Charles Mingus' jazz to 1970s-era salsa and Tejano folk music. He is currently working on a book about the craze for hillbilly and race records in the 1920s. He and his Kramer appear regularly at an Austin club near you.

  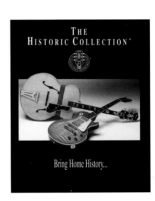

Admit it. The word *pickup* makes you think "single-coil or humbucker?" A *neck* has frets. *Action* is something you lower. You are a gearhead. Most guitarists I've met are. We spend more time talking equipment than counterpoint. We are seduced by cutaway curves. Sixty-cycle hum—however diligently we suppress it—is a warm, soothing bath. And at one point, each of us has said something like "That new stomp box is going to make all the difference." A big part of playing guitar is discussing the guitars we play. Music is in the material. Guitars can be dear friends, tormentors, or mere tools of the trade. Quite often they are advertisements for ourselves.

Not all gearheads are the same. Sure, we all succumb to the telltale fetish: Outer beauty reflects inner virtue. But we do not kneel in the same way. Gearheads come in three distinct varieties. I am sure you have met them all.

First, the technophile. This gearhead has an unshakeable belief in progress. The latest is the best. Improvements have been made, features added, or fashion thrust forward. The most commonly identified gearhead, the technophile propels industry

NO BOZOS
A Kramer with Floyd Rose tremolo was the ultimate 1980s gear for the non-gearhead.

innovation for its own sake—with rather mixed results. Technophiles bought the first Explorers. They owned Ovations.

Second, the God-fearing atheist. On the surface, this gearhead rejects everything the technophile holds dear. He plays junk. He scoffs at equipment talk. He proves one can make beautiful music with an ugly rig. Think Bird blasting "Ko Ko" on a plastic horn. The sneaky God-fearing atheist insists he is not a gearhead. But do not be taken by his ruse. He protests too much.

The God-fearing atheist is just as caught in the equipment trap as is the technophile.

Third, the historian. Growing in number, the historian is a hybrid. He combines the technophile's attention to detail with the atheist's rejection of progress. His favorite word is "vintage." Things ain't what they used to be. Historians like what is old. Some have been witnessed paying astronomical prices for technophiles' former fetishes. Others champion yesterday's detritus, believing it is far cooler to play

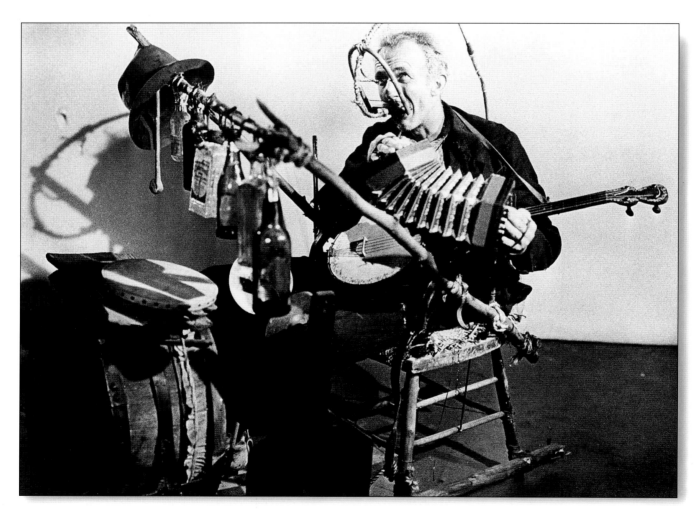

THE ULTIMATE GEARHEAD
A one-man-band maestro plays his banjo, complete with full effects rack.

GIBSON ELECTRIC TRIO
Opposite page: In 1953, Gibson tentatively unveiled its Les Paul Standard solid body. Then, in 1957, the firm announced the Flying V, without doubt one of the most radical guitar shapes ever. Gibson had gone from staid to outlandish in just a few short years. But solid-body electrics didn't fare too well at Gibson in the 1950s, and only ninety-eight Flying Vs were sold in 1958–1959. This 1959 Flying V is flanked by a Les Paul Custom and Standard and stands before a 1950s Gibson GA-40 Les Paul amp. Owner: Brian Fischer. (Photograph © *Vintage Guitar*)

guitars rejected by their parents' generation than those dismissed by their own.

How do I know all this? What gives me the right to define the gearhead world? One simple fact: I am the original owner of a 1984 Kramer Pacer Deluxe with Candy Apple Red custom finish, Floyd Rose locking tremolo system, Seymour Duncan humbucker pickup, two EMG active single coils, unfinished neck, beefy frets, and even a handy dual allen wrench holder mounted on the back of the headstock. This has been my only guitar for almost twenty years. It has given me two important windows into the gearhead.

First, my Kramer has the special power to reveal the inner gearhead. Players respond strongly. What was your reaction when you read the word *Kramer*? Did you swoon? Did you feel sorry for me? Did you quickly flip through this book to find a soothing sunburst Les Paul? Tell me what you think of my Kramer, and I'll tell you what kind of gearhead you are.

Second, my long relationship with my Kramer has carried me through the full gamut of the equipment fetish experience. Technophile, God-fearing atheist, historian: I have lived them all. Let me tell you the story of my tumultuous affair with my Kramer Pacer Deluxe. It started well before the guitar even existed.

My guitar teacher told me rock was the Devil's music. Thirteen in central Texas, I did not know enough to prove him wrong. The western swing guru had guided me well so far. From Maybelle Carter's "Wildwood Flower" through Bob Wills, Chet Atkins, and even dumbed-down Jazz Messengers, he instilled an early appreciation of harmony, counterpoint, and manual dexterity. I knew how to play a minor 7 flat 5 before I had even heard of a power chord. I was a freak.

At least I knew I was missing something. I pushed him into a compromise with Bob Seger. But even I understood "Old Time Rock and Roll" was nothing but Chuck Berry sapped of rebellion, a 1978 nostalgia salve for those under siege by music dangerous in all the wrong ways. Punk exposed doughy arena rock fans. Disco outed straight guys' inner squares. And Van Halen, exploding from the Pasadena yard-party scene, declared metal was more than plodding primitivism. There was rebellion, even joy, in virtuosity. I was hooked. I quit the lessons soon after hearing "Ice Cream Man."

Thus began my teenage obsession with Van Halen. The band quickly became the center of my own private folk tradition. I imbibed all the information I could. Album grooves wore thin. Magazines and "Dr. Licks" transcription books filled my mailbox. Could I play the stuff? No. But that didn't stop me. I wasn't very good at Seger tunes either.

Finger-tapping arpeggios may have been an odd entry into rock and roll, but I did not know it at the time. I devoured "Eruption" with the same hunger I read Eddie had for Clapton's "Crossroads" solo—and for some of the same reasons. Here was music both familiar and strange. Unlike their metal peers, Van Halen swung. The band's groove—progeny of the Stones' R&B or even Aerosmith's boogie—eased me away from my disco singles. To my ears, "So This is Love" shared something with "Shake Your Groove Thing." Hey, I was thirteen. They both got me dancing. Yet Eddie's pyrotechnics catapulted the music to new heights—the blues on steroids. He took what I knew and made it better than I imagined. It was like nothing I had ever heard. Speed. Technique. Drama. Eddie was an accomplished gymnast. I worshiped his athleticism. I coveted his gear.

But it could not be had. Van Halen's early discs featured guitars that had seen far more tearing apart than putting back together. A miscellaneous neck bolted to a Strat-style body with a single humbucker. That's it. You could not pick up one of these at the store. To my utter amazement, Eddie did not talk stock guitars and gear when interviewed by guitar magazines. Gearheads know. *Every* feature in a guitar magazine reads like an infomercial: generic guitar hero plays X guitar, Y amp, Z strings, ABCDEF effects boxes, etc. The message is clear. If you want to play like your idol, put your cash on the barrelhead. Rather than dropping brand names, Eddie filled early interviews with lists of spare parts. On early tours he packed three or four guitar bodies, ten extra necks, and a variety of tremolo systems. It was an affront to the gear fetish code. In Guitar Town, USA, Van Halen was the tenant who

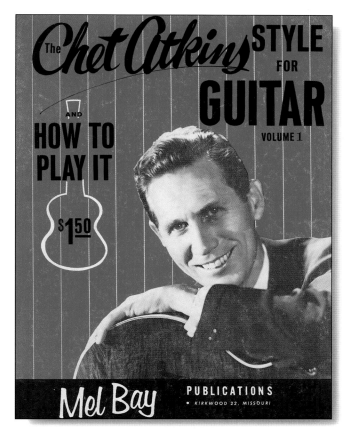

CHET ATKINS 1962 METHOD BOOK

1960 GRETSCH CHET ATKINS MODEL 6120
Opposite page: During the 1950s and 1960s, Gretsch built the Cadillac of guitars—lots of chrome, lots of tone. And if Gretsch could have figured out how to add tailfins to a guitar, they probably would have. Working with Gretsch's traditional Streamliner hollow body and electrics, Chet Atkins tailored the 6120 to his liking. Gretsch designers then dressed the first 1955 6120s up in cowboy duds, from the glorious woodburned G-brand to the western-motif fretboard inlays. The look was a little too outlandish for Atkins and was deleted from subsequent 1957 and later versions. Owner: Karl Dixon. (Photograph © *Vintage Guitar*)

kept broken cars in his yard just in case he needed the parts. While others complained about the property values, Eddie created mongrel hot rods far superior to the stock models. It was a cruel joke. For a young kid like me, his equipment was as unobtainable as his technique. It was also a liberation. Eddie inspired my early gearhead atheism.

Freed from the gear trap, I jumped into the music itself. My friend dreamed endlessly about the pristine white Les Paul at the local music store. He would lie down on my bed, stare at the ceiling, and weave detailed odes to this distant, untouchable lover. Everything would be different once he owned that guitar. While he waxed, I practiced. Pentatonic riffs. Scales in every position, every permutation I could think of. Chord inversions. I knew my Phrygian from my Mixolydian. Music was spiritual. It was about combining sound and technique, desire and discipline. He just didn't get it. He was more into consumption than music. He was a sucker.

Eddie would know what I was talking about, I insisted. He was just like me. He recalled his teenage years in countless interviews. His brother Alex would invite him out to parties, but Eddie preferred to stay home alone with his guitar. When his brother returned at 3 A.M., Eddie would still be sitting on the side of his bed with his guitar in his hands. Joy came from practice, not parties. I sucked up these accounts of my hero's teen dedication. They validated my so-called life. He could have been describing any one of my countless weekend nights—well, except that part about being invited to parties. I practiced. A lot. My crappy guitar let everyone see that I knew what music was all about. I wore it with pride.

Then everything changed. Eddie became a pitchman. He had held out longer than most. The award-winning young gun must have been seen as the Holy Grail of endorsers within the industry—a wildly popular musician with a mountain of street credibility

based on his monster technique and previous refusal to sell out. Getting him on board was money in the bank. Kramer did it.

At the time Van Halen released their first album, Kramer looked like the least likely candidate to become the world's top guitar company. Kramer was born in early 1976, as Travis Bean employee Gary Kramer decided that one company manufacturing aluminum-necked guitars was not enough. Finding backers, Kramer rolled its first guitar off the line later that year. Early Kramers featured aluminum necks inlayed with strips of wood. They supposedly kept the sustain and bright tones of the Bean while more closely approximating the feel of a traditional guitar. They were also a lot cheaper. They sold reasonably well for oddballs, and Kramer established itself as a respectable sidebar in the story of twentieth-century guitar lore—"Remember those wacky aluminum-necked Kramers?" The company wanted more. With the explosion of the metal scene in the early Eighties, Kramer found its new calling. Perhaps they were inspired by the popularity of Eddie's striped mongrels. Along with upstarts Charvel and Jackson, Kramer began slapping humbuckers into Strat-styled solidbodies. Oh yeah, the new Kramers also featured necks made of wood.

Kramer would not have gotten very far without Floyd Rose. Floyd was a mulleted guitarist and inventor who dreamed of staying in tune after wammy-bar dive bombs. By the late Seventies, he had developed a new system that did the trick by locking down the strings at the nut and bridge. He could wiggle his Floyd Rose tremolo violently and the guitar would stay in perfect tune—for weeks. Guitar companies scoffed. He couldn't sell his invention to any of them. Frustrated, Floyd contacted Eddie. Who better? Van Halen had already talked about his elaborate techniques for popping his strings back in tune after wammy workouts: wanking individual strings, slapping the headstock—everything short of prayer. Eddie was

1965 RICKENBACKER 360/12
Rickenbacker launched its novel twelve-string electric at the dawn of the 1960s and was bolstered when George Harrison began playing one with The Beatles. The Rick twelve-string went on to create the "jingle-jangle" sound of The Byrds' version of Bob Dylan's "Mr. Tambourine Man" to become forever associated with 1960s pop. This new-style Mapleglo 360/12 is surrounded by a variety of Fireglo Ricks. Owner: Mike Tamborrino. (Photograph © *Vintage Guitar*)

BRITISH GEAR
British-made Zemaitis guitars lean against a Mini Cooper S. Cabinetmaker Tony Zemaitis turned to building guitars in the 1960s, and his creations soon caught the eyes of the English rock intelligentsia, from Donovan to George Harrison, Ron Wood to Eric Clapton. Zemaitis became famed for his engraved, metal-fronted electrics, which now rank among the most valuable guitar gear anywhere. Owner: Keith Smart. (Photograph © *Vintage Guitar*)

impressed. Tinny tone aside, the Floyd Rose only went out of tune when he jumped off speaker stacks and shifted the neck. Not bad. Eddie was enough to get Rose in the door. Rose ran into a Kramer exec, again pushed his product, and promised to bring Eddie around. Kramer bought it all. Within a few years, Kramer penned an exclusive with Floyd Rose and got Eddie too. I was about to be hooked.

The ad that turned me into a technophile didn't even feature my favorite guitarist. Sure, I had already heard about Eddie's love for the Floyd Rose. I knew his growing interest in Kramers. But the one that got me was pure commodity. A pristine picture of a Pacer Deluxe. Candy Apple against black background. Floyd floating over the shiny finish and smooth contours. It was a seduction. I tore the ad out of the magazine. I hung it on my wall. I took it down and held it. The guitar filled my dreams. I could hear it in my head. The guitar spoke to everything I thought I knew about making music. Beauty. Control. Disciplined abandon. Skill supported by technology. I knew I was being had. I didn't care.

I told everyone about my Pacer. Parents. Brother. Friends. My Les Paul lover wasn't hearing it. I had chided him before he got his dream rig. Now I fell for the fetish and wanted his sympathy? For a Kramer? He thought I was crazy. I was just hungry.

Eddie started showing up in ads. "It's very simply the best guitar you can buy today." This did not help. His ads confirmed many of my ideas about the man. He was comfortable, casual in his stance. He wore street clothes. His T-shirt declared "No Bozos." For me, this was an indictment of everything I had learned to loath about most metal acts: the manufactured masculinity, the crass sexism, and above all the doom and gloom. Why were all the metal bands so mean and angry? I didn't buy it. It was just a game. Eddie wasn't playing. He was down to earth, focused on the music. Even more, Eddie found guitar playing fun. He joked. He smiled rather than grimaced. All this appealed to how I wanted to be. It all got represented in that sweet ad on my wall.

It took me over a year to find the guitar. I looked everywhere. San Antonio. Austin. Houston. Mail order attempts failed. Outfits went out of business between order and delivery. I waited. I almost gave up. Stepping into a shop to buy some strings, I saw it on the wall. I was floored. I bought it the next day.

As always, the gearhead dream died with the gear reality. The Pacer in my hands was beautiful, but it failed to live up to my unreal expectations. It sounded like my fingers, not my fantasies. Still, it was a great axe. The smooth neck. The humbucker crunch. Those effortless distorted bombs. Playing the Kramer was fun. I smiled.

I lost interest in Van Halen. Not long after playing "Jump" in the high school talent show, my ears moved on to other sounds—many influenced by what I learned under Eddie's wing. I slowly shifted toward the fusion wails of Jeff Beck covering "Cause We've Ended As Lovers." Through Al Di Meola's speed typing. Into McLaughlin and Scofield dropping Miles' tri-tone blues. I even started listening to musicians who didn't play the guitar. The Kramer carried me. It was no longer the dream axe, but it was good enough to take me where I wanted. Kramers by this time were nothing remarkable. Everyone played them. They were the best selling guitars in America.

It wasn't until punk broke that my guitar needed fixing. Nirvana made the world safe for historians. Technophiles were suddenly jokes laughed off of MTV. I held fast. Part of it was money. Part pride. My supreme techno-fetish—now out of favor—became a symbol of my returning atheism. I vowed to make relevant music with an Eighties cliché. People first shook their heads. Bandmates and friends sported Jaguars, Rickenbackers, and Teles. They considered me a loser the moment they saw my guitar. A leisure suit in the middle of "A Hard Day's Night." Or was it "Pink Flamingos" at Cannes? I loved it. My dream guitar had become my favorite joke. It was beginning to identify gearheads.

Just a few years ago, things changed again. I never thought I'd see it happen. It was slow at first—almost imperceptible. My band was booked into a generic Austin club: post-punk, alt-country, emo, shoegazing scene. The vibe was moody, a limp "Nevermind." Not the Eighties' "Kill 'Em All," but joy was just as far away. The sound guy was an asshole. I had played the club a few weeks before on a borrowed guitar. This time the man refused to acknowledge my presence even when I called him by name. His demeanor changed instantly as I drew my battered Kramer out of its case. A broad smile crossed his hardened face. The man got giddy. He began gushing about his first guitar, a Kramer Baretta. I was an instant friend. I legitimated this guy's secret past. I even took it on stage.

I was soon finding closet Kramer fans everywhere I went. Hipsters came up to me and talked. Snickers turned to whispered confessions then wide-grinned ease. Shame evaporated into relief. Soon vintage freaks felt free to embrace their teen technophilia. I heard about Steinbergers, Roland synth guitars, more than I wanted to know. Historians who maintained a decorous, almost bored respect when discussing their quest for a '57 Les Paul or '63 Tele, broke free when talking about their early drive for a Warlock. My Kramer was a therapist—one that went out of tune every time I leapt from a speaker cabinet.

I recently bought a new guitar—a Heritage 335 copy. It sounds better than any Gibson I've played but still gets the quizzical stares familiar to my Pacer. Made by Gibson luthiers who didn't go along with Gibson's new transnational facelift, the Heritage allows me to embrace both my historian and my atheist. The technophile still lurks below. One never escapes the gearhead within. Once activated, it remains. But twelve steps are not necessary. All that is required is the embrace of the urge. Once held close, the gearhead can coexist peacefully with that more important urge to create music that matters.

Here is my twenty-year story of the evolution of a gearhead—my desire to make music and my descent into gear fetishism. Let it be a lesson to all. I will see you each soon at the next guitar show—my first. I'll be the one walking past the Fenders, Stellas, and Gibsons with my new vintage-status Kramer Pacer Deluxe. Just try to stare into its Candy Apple Red custom finish and tell me you're not a gearhead.

The Male Guitar Hormone and You

How to Find True Love on Six Strings— And Not Be Treated Like a Stompbox!

By Sigrid Arnott

Ms. Arnott is a regular correspondent for Elle Guitar *and* Ladies Guitar Journal. *Her articles have explored all aspects of guitar relationships from care to beauty. Recent articles include "Guitar Makeovers: Refinishing Tips From Hot Rockers"; "Getting Him to Put Down Your Axe"; "Is Your Band in the Way of Your Life?" and "Guitar Techniques Sure to Turn Him On."*

Scientists have yet to discover, name, and study the human male hormone that regulates the desire for guitars and gear, but ask most any woman and she can tell you all about it. Women also know this hormone is linked to a gene that regulates gender relations—a.k.a. the Girlfriend Gene. As a teenage boy reaches a certain point in his development, chemicals enter (or more often, flood) his brain creating simultaneous signals that he needs an electric guitar and wants a girlfriend. Of course, we all confuse needs and wants and in this case the confusion is often expressed as: "I need a guitar to get the girlfriend I want."

Just so you can try to fathom what he's going through, here's how things often play out.

1958 GIBSON EXPLORER

Gibson was always a rather sober company in its early days. And then suddenly, in 1957, the firm announced its Modernistic Guitars, including the Flying V, Explorer, and the Futura, which never saw the light of day. If the Stratocaster's body shape was radically curvaceous, these new Gibson solid bodies were daringly geometric. In fact, they might have been too daring, as only about thirty-eight Explorers were built in 1958–1959. Owner: Larry Briggs. (Photograph © *Vintage Guitar*)

UKULELE LADY
Nothing was more beguiling than a full moon over the volcano and the soft sounds of a uke.

Yearnings, desire, hot and cold sensations . . . soon pin-ups of gorgeous, sexy guitars clad in Purple Passion or Baby Doll Blue paint jobs appear on the bedroom walls of the young man in question. The hormone that creates this desire is elevated by glossy guitar pornography magazines with Neon Green or Blaze Orange headlines that wail, "Your Axe in 2005!" "Humbuckers or Single Coils: What Rocks *You*?" or "Boost your Amp . . . Today!" The desire for a guitar becomes urgent.

At some point during this painful process, you enter the scene, innocent and unsuspecting. Maybe you and he talk about music, and you think he's artistic or interesting or in vague need of your love and guidance. We don't know what he thinks and, most likely, he doesn't either.

When girls get emotionally confused, we get on the phone. When guys experience emotion, they get the urge to be in a band. The same young man who can't manage to verbalize (in an intimate setting) a sentence such as, "Uh, I kinda like you," will scream sentimental love songs at top amplified volume to large groups of strangers. These audiences might include you and the message might be aimed at you, but the public nature of the emotional release moves the message away from *conversation* and into the less-threatening sphere of *performance*.

At this time, our young man has a revelation: He has to play a guitar in a band to win you over. The first step, he thinks, is to get the guitar.

All the guy really wants at this point is something that looks like the axe his guitar hero plays, but a guitar is *gear* and gear needs to be exhaustively researched from qualitative and quantitative perspectives. The same magazines that fed the original desire now feed the guitar obsession. The guy can escape the emotional upheavals caused by thinking about the upcoming quest to form a band and play for you by delving into exciting guitar topics like "String-Scorching Solos!" "In Pursuit of Pickup Polarity Perfection!" "Discover Double-Digit Distortion!" and "The Legend of Leo!" A new language—that of *guitar lore*—must be learned before the novice heads out on the path to the guitar store.

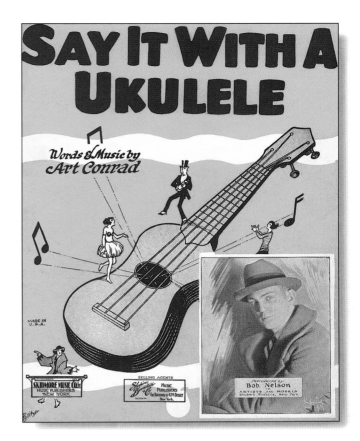

"SAY IT WITH A UKULELE"
L'amour was always best said with a uke.

Things often hit a snag here for the simple reason that the guy now realizes he might need to actually be able to *play* a guitar in order to "test" axes. Now, some guitar, any guitar, even an *acoustic* guitar, must be found—perhaps one dating to the time in the distant past when our proto-guitar hero's father "needed" a guitar. Somehow the guy figures out how to fret the intro licks to some complex anthem—remember, playing simple chords to a beat comes much later in a young man's musical education.

At the same time, things have been progressing with you. While he was agonizing over his future axe, you have been playing mental reruns of the time you sat together listening to a song. While he was grooving to some guitar riffs, you heard, or misheard, "Ooh Ooh baby, I Loo-ove you." Thus, when he said it was a cool song, you thought, "He likes me!" Unwittingly, he has formed a one-person potential audience.

Now, in preparation for advancement to the guitar-testing level of the quest, he strums that borrowed guitar for you. When you're there, he practices playing cool yet complex phrases without making strange facial grimaces. You naturally get bored and casually pick up whatever reading material is left laying about—usually a guitar rag. Often you find that puzzling over wiring circuits and the pros and cons of three- versus five-way selector switches is more soothing than reading the anxiety-producing articles on thigh management you are used to pondering in *TeenBeautiful Magazine*. Times passes, and when you get really bored and say, "That's great!"—meaning "You can stop now!"—he believes your words and a great misunderstanding is born.

The guy now imagines the ecstasy you will mutually enjoy as he performs finger-burning arpeggios on his [insert current dream guitar here] for you. In this fantasy, colored lights flash through the dark, steamy venue and across his body/axe. As he looks down upon the surging crowd of fans, you, the faithful girlfriend, advance toward him. You seem to be trying to tell him something over the roar of his seven-minute long shredding solo. He focuses harder on your lips, finally understanding you: "I love . . . your . . . playing."

Now all the elements are in place for the guitar quest: 1) the ability to say simple key phrases like "zebra-humbucker Les Paul" or "solid-body Fender"; 2) the facility to play a musical phrase; and 3) a guitar fantasy to ease the excitement and anxiety caused by the whole project.

Trips are made to guitar stores, probably with another guy sharing emerging interests in the opposite sex, exotic guitar gear, and the world of banddom. This is a personal time in a young man's life and you must treat it with the respect for privacy it deserves. Stay away! Women who have been brought on these trips find they are unbelievably time-consuming and tedious. It's not even really *shopping* because nothing is actually purchased! If you are forced to suffer Post-Traumatic Guitar Boredom Syndrome, all you can hope for is to suppress all memories of these events.

Although you will usually manage to escape these trips, you must always be there to listen to him pour out his feelings about the possible purchase. He calls you to share his anguish. He doesn't know if he should buy the Bulgarian copy-cat of the 1957 Stratocaster (the uncoveted Balkancaster), a re-refinished reissue of a classic Gibson SG in 1970 Dodge Charger Hemi metalflake purple with a neck scalloped à la Yngwie Malmsteen, or a semi-hollow, semi-dented Gretsch with homemade wood-burned cattle-brands? All of a sudden it seems that taking home just one guitar will be like sacrificing another guitar to an unworthy guitar owner who might not rehabilitate it through his love.

And buying only one dream guitar will prevent him from living out other guitar dreams. If he buys the left-handed, right-strung Strat copy, he could rock like Hendrix but will never be able to play like Chet Atkins on his Gretsch. What had seemed like a simple proposition of choosing the most guitar features for the least amount of cash is now the horrible problem of discarding one musical triumph in exchange for the dubious possibility of attaining another.

Then you inevitably ask what the favored guitar costs and the real trouble begins. First off, he doesn't think you will approve of any purchase price greater than $50, so he has to do mental gymnastics to convert all prices to 1970s-era currency. Secondly, he never noticed your bored perusals of his guitar magazines so he misunderstands your sincere interest in guitar pricing as a harsh economical perspective that sees the instrument purchase as little more than a simple commercial transaction and not a life-changing transformation.

Worst of all, you start to correct his guitar facts and you point out that for the style of music you thought he liked, he will never want the tone produced by Dynosonic pickups in a semi-hollow body, that refinished reissues have no resale value, or that the tone-pot wiring in Bulgarian electrics comes from Soviet Army surplus and always produces nasty feedback. Our young man experiences an empty hole

POWER TRIO
Sweet sounds and romantic riffs were the domain of this fiddle, accordion, and guitar power trio.

FENDER STRATOCASTER DUO
While on the Esquire and Telecaster it came stock, blond was an extra-cost custom color for Stratocasters but one that many owners chose, making it the secondmost popular Strat finish after sunburst. This blonde dates from 1958. Olympic White was the next step brighter, as on this left-handed 1962—a guitar that Jimi Hendrix would have appreciated. Owner: Craig Brody. (Photograph © *Vintage Guitar*)

growing in his lower abdomen as you begin to rant about the glories of pre-CBS technology.

When you ask him how he intends to amplify his guitar and his stance on vacuum tubes versus solid-state and Class A compared to Class B wiring, he decides it's not a good time to tell you he was hoping you would buy him the amp as a retroactive birthday present (from before you met).

How can he tell you that as he contemplated the high cost of achieving male maturity in America, he

was hoping that you might break into your babysitting savings or get an extra job to foot the bill? Learning to play the guitar, forming a band, beginning the endless search for a reliable drummer, buying equipment and gigs—all to win your love and admiration—will be time-consuming and expensive. How can he explain the epiphany he experienced when he realized that he needs a girlfriend to get him what he wants—a guitar.

In the end, caution is always advised when dealing with electric guitars in human relationships.

FIRST BANDS

"We were a smokin' band. Boy, I mean we would set fire to a building in a second. We were just up there blowing as funky as we pleased. Sixteen years old, forty-one dollars a week. Big time."
—Duane Allman on his first band, The Houserockers, quoted in Scott Freeman's *Midnight Riders: The Story of the Allman Brothers Band*

"The first band I was ever in was in fifth grade. We played along with records, miming the music. I sang at a student convocation in seventh grade. Me and a guy named Sam Abbott did the song 'Abilene.' He played guitar, I sang, and this other kid played congas. It was horrible. But the first real band I joined was Crepe Soul. I was in that band for a year and a half. I decided bands don't work, this idea of everybody voting on everything, because nothing ever got done and we never played anyplace. After I quit Crepe Soul, I joined a band called Snakepit Banana Barn and got kicked out because I couldn't sing. Then I bought an acoustic guitar and just started playing songs. I even told my mom and dad I wrote Donovan's 'Universal Soldier.'"
—John Cougar Mellencamp, *The Rolling Stone Interviews: The 1980s*

"Steve Ross, a friend who played guitar in the first garage band I was in (and would be an important friend for many years to come), turned me on to guitar. We could jam on a basic blues or a Hendrix number for an hour and a half at a time. I'm sure it stunk, but to us it was the stuff."
—David Cassidy, *C'mon, Get Happy . . .*

REC ROOM ROCKERS
Armed with his Sears, Roebuck mail-order Silvertone, a young guitarman plays the blues.

HARD ROCKERS
The versatile Nevinaires pose for a publicity still.

CHAPTER 2

Legends

FAITHFUL AUDIENCE
Music and screen star Guy Mitchell strums his guitar for the
one audience you can always trust to appreciate your music.

REPUBLIC PICTURES presents
GENE AUTRY
in
"The SINGING COWBOY"
with SMILEY BURNETTE
and "CHAMPION"
DIRECTED BY MACK WRIGHT
SUPERVISED BY ARMAND SCHAEFER
SCREENPLAY BY DORRELL and STUART McGOWAN
ORIGINAL STORY BY TOM GIBSON
Produced by NAT LEVINE
REPUBLIC PICTURES
A REPUBLIC PICTURE

The Singing Cowboy's Guitar
His Best Friend . . . After His Horse
By Douglas B. Green

Ranger Doug—a.k.a. Douglas B. Green—is the Idol of American Youth and the founder of Riders in the Sky, an old-time band of good comedy, stellar harmony, and mighty fine family entertainment that has released more than twenty albums of western music. He is a guitarist, composer, and singer who can yodel like there's no tomorrow. Doug is also a renowned music historian with a master's degree in literature. He is the author Singing in the Saddle: The History of the Singing Cowboy. *This essay tells the tale of the first guitar heroes—the singing cowboys of TV and movie fame that inspired generations to pick up guitars and play.*

There is no more enduring image of the old west as fixed in our minds by countless westerns than that of a cowboy singing a song while strumming his faithful old guitar around the campfire, joining the band at the barn dance, serenading the school marm on the front porch, or yodeling as he rides on horseback. It is as much a part of how we think of, say, Gene Autry or Roy Rogers as is his hat, his floral shirt, or even Champion or Trigger. It will ever be the way we think of the cowboy and song.

Is there any basis in reality? Not much. The "parlor guitars" of the late nineteenth century, the era of the great trail drives, while small by today's standards, were too bulky for horseback or chuck wagon, and too fragile and too susceptible to the extremes of weather and temperature to have been used much in historical cowboy days, although a few did doubtless find their way to bunkhouses and line camps a hundred and more years ago. A more likely instrument was the banjo, then common due to the ubiquitously popular minstrel shows. Yet it too took up space and was sensitive to weather and shock.

"THE SINGING COWBOY"
Gene Autry was the quintessential singing cowboy—and he could really sing and play his guitar!

More common yet was the fiddle, the true folk instrument of the frontier, but it is evident that as far as the trail drives go, the cowboy overwhelming had no instrument at all to support whatever singing he did.

But the image was fixed early. When concert singer Bentley Ball recorded several cowboy songs for Victor in 1919 as part of a collection of folk songs, he strummed a guitar. And by the time the earliest cowboy singers like Vernon Dalhart, John I. White, Carson J. Robison, and others made it to record in the mid 1920s, all either played or were supported prominently by the guitar. While there had been earlier hits on Broadway like "My Pony Boy" and "Ragtime Cowboy Joe," no one, not even then, associated the

ROY ROGERS
Roy *sans* guitar but with his famous faithful steed, Trigger.

SINGING COWBOY HEROES
Opposite page: Lil' Tex is all worn out from riding with the posse, but a song from his first guitar hero will put some bounce back in his boots.

piano or orchestra with cowboy song. The guitar was fixed in our consciousness as the cowboy's instrument of choice.

If there was any ambivalence about this before, this image was fixed by film. When *In Old Arizona* was released in 1929 it became not only the first western to feature sound, but also the first to feature music: Warner Baxter (who won an academy award for his portrayal of the Cisco Kid in this film) serenades his lovely costar Dorothy Burgess playing a tenor guitar.

Few of the rough, tough he-men who made early westerns were actually musical. The one big exception was Ken Maynard, the best rider of them all, who played passable guitar and fiddle and sang in several of his early westerns, having been at the premier of *In Old Arizona* and being convinced that his audience would welcome musical interludes. Others, including Bob Steele, a very young John Wayne (with voice dubbed by Bill Bradbury), and even Colonel Tim McCoy sang a snatch or two of a song on film, but though the seed had been planted, the flower didn't bloom until a young radio singer named Gene Autry made a guest appearance in a Ken Maynard film called *In Old Santa Fe*. The young radio star with his megawatt smile and guileless, likable manner, was an immediate hit with audiences nationwide, and a whole film genre was born. The inexperienced youngster was quickly thrust into starring roles at the newly formed Republic Pictures, and became a national sensation. He was not big and strapping like Maynard, George O'Brien, or Buck Jones, nor even compactly muscular like Tom Mix; instead he was as likely to settle arguments with reason or a sweet song, and although there were the requisite thrills and chases in his movies, he won over a whole new audience with his gentle comic byplay with Smiley Burnette and his winning voice. And all the while he strummed his beautiful mother-of-pearl-decorated Martin D-45, one of many exquisitely rare and beautiful guitars he would own in his long lifetime.

Autry quickly made a great deal of money for Republic, and others in Hollywood were quick to recognize and reinforce a trend. In fact, Warner Brothers released its first singing cowboy western,

starring handsome pop vocalist Dick Foran, in November 1935, just a month after Autry's first starring picture, suggesting the idea had occurred to more studio than one; midsize, efficiency-minded Republic was simply the first to get this new product to market. In the years that followed, every major and minor studio (with the exception of MGM, who probably felt it had its quota of outdoor singers filled with Nelson Eddy) offered a series of singing cowboy pictures: Spectrum with Fred Scott, Grand National with Tex Ritter, RKO with Ray Whitley, Universal with Bob Baker, Monogram with Jack Randall, 20th Century-Fox with Smith Ballew, and the young Sons of the Pioneers featured prominently in the Charles Starrett series at Columbia. One of the Pioneers stepped out of the band to become Republic's second singing cowboy, Roy Rogers. There were many more, of course, singers who made a single film like Art Jarrett, Tex Fletcher, or Gene Austin, and several historically fascinating experiments like the all-black cast singing cowboy films of Herb Jeffries, or Grand National's singing cowgirl series starring Dorothy Page.

The war years brought another, younger posse of singers to the screen: Jimmy Wakely at Monogram, Ken Curtis at Columbia, and Eddie Dean at PRC, Republic, which continued to enjoy the most success with the singing cowboy film, developed two more stars: Monte Hale and Rex Allen.

It was, as one would expect, the singers with folk or country backgrounds who were the guitarists and were prominently featured with their instruments: Autry, Rogers, Ritter, Whitley, Wakely, and Dean. Oddly enough, the singers drawn from the light opera talent pool like George Houston and Fred Scott often posed with guitars, but did not really play them; they simply chorded (or faked chording) to the soundtrack. Interestingly it was the pop singers like Foran and Donald Grayson who didn't pretend to play, although they were, of course, supported by a sidekick or band strumming guitars.

And oh, the guitars they played! Autry had a collection of pearl-bound Martins of all sizes. Roy Rogers proudly played his Martin OM-45 Deluxe, though he was later seen with a Martin D-28 and a Gibson Super 400 as well. Ray Whitley's custom Gibson J-200 intrigued his fellow singing stars Jimmy Wakely, Tex Ritter, and Autry as well, and all were seen playing these rosewood beauties in film and on stage. Bob Baker played a beautiful Gibson Advanced Jumbo, while others like Eddie Dean, Johnny Bond, and Rex Allen favored the simple elegance of the Martin D-28. Autry, Allen, Patsy Montana, and Lloyd Perryman of the Sons of the Pioneers, all of whom had had connections to Chicago in their careers, also owned beautiful pearl-inlaid guitars made by the Larson Brothers (made under a variety of names) in the Windy City. Archtop orchestra guitars were not featured as much, but those who played them played good ones indeed: Wesley Tuttle and Jerry Scoggins of the Cass County Boys both played blonde Gibson L-5s (and, though they are well into their eighties, still do so today!) while Gene Monbeck, a small man, was nearly dwarfed by his huge Stromberg Master 400 in his many years with the Whippoorwills. In my own work with Riders in the Sky, I've always favored the archtop for swing rhythm, playing a 1939 Gibson L-5 cutaway until it was stolen, then a couple of wonderful Triggs guitars made in the 1980s and 1990s, and more lately one of several Strombergs, the ultimate rhythm guitar.

In the 1930s, cowboy songs were all over the airwaves. Boston-born erstwhile westerner Billy Hill wrote Broadway hits with a western theme like "The Last Round-Up" and "Empty Saddles In The Old Corral," and they quickly became sensations in the country field. Gene Autry recorded hit after hit for Columbia in this era, including million sellers like "That Silver Haired Daddy of Mine," "Yellow Rose of Texas," "South of the Border," "Mexicali Rose," "Back In The Saddle Again," and "You Are My Sunshine." And while no other western artist approached this record of success, Roy Rogers, Tex Ritter, and the Sons

SINGING COWGIRL
Even cowgirls can sing the blues. Songstress Nellie Brown duded up in rhinestones and guitar to sing about the good old Wild West.

FENDER ESQUIRE AND TELECASTER CUSTOM-COLOR QUARTET
Custom-color pre-CBS Telecasters are rarities but iridescent Esquires are nearly impossible to find. Most buyers willing to pay for color also anteed up for the neck pickup. The Custom Esquire, left center, came stock in sunburst, however. Owner: Larry Henderson/Ax in Hand. (Photograph © *Vintage Guitar*)

of the Pioneers made memorable popular and western music in the years before World War Two. Nearly every radio station in the country had a western show or two, featuring either local cowboy singers or transcribed programs by the top stars. Of course Rogers and Autry both had long running network radio shows.

The coming of war brought an end to the halcyon era of the singing cowboy. Not only do all national musical fads bloom and fade in their time, but the grim reality of the bloody world war made the sunny, musical Depression-era fantasies seem unrealistic; most films became less escapist, more hard-edged, and though the genre was popular enough to sustain itself and even develop new stars in the 1940s, the handwriting was on the wall. Tex Ritter made his last starring western in 1945, Roy Rogers in 1951, Gene Autry in 1953, and Rex Allen made the last of its kind in 1954.

Likewise the music of the west was heard less and less. Tex Ritter and Jimmy Wakely were huge record sellers, but primarily with country music; Roy Rogers with children's music, and Gene Autry developed a whole new career as a singer of seasonal songs like "Here Comes Santa Claus" and the biggest selling record of his career, "Rudolph, The Red-Nosed Reindeer." Only Tex Ritter's haunting "Do Not Forsake Me" from the film *High Noon*, and big bandleader Vaughn Monroe's driving "Riders In The Sky" stand out as western hits from the 1950s.

That is, until country singer Marty Robbins, who had grown up in the thrall of singing cowboys, had a surprising string of western hits during the early years of rock and roll, including "El Paso," "Big Iron," and "Five Brothers," all featuring the fluid, rollicking guitar (played on a gut-string classical with a flat pick) of Grady Martin. A series of gunfighter ballads and trail songs albums were extremely popular, but only a part of the huge and varied body of work Robbins created, singing calypso, rockabilly, pop, country, folk, and Hawaiian music in his long career.

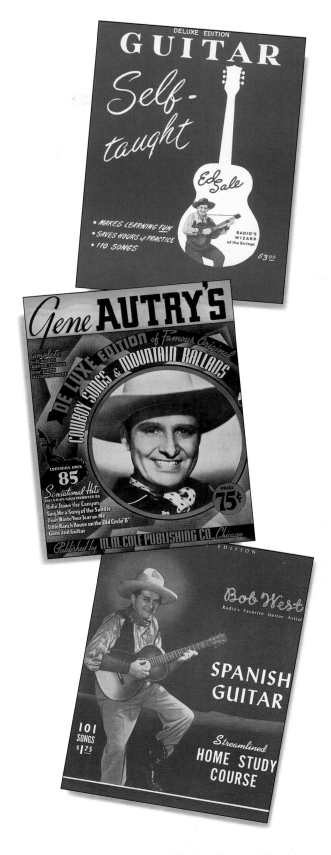

COWGIRL CHORUSLINE
Opposite page: Cowgirls Verna and Verda Rodik strummed their guitars out on the range in 1941's *The Return of Daniel Boone.*

1956 GRETSCH CHET ATKINS MODEL 6120
From its G-brand on the bass bout to the longhorn on the headstock, Gretsch's first Model 6120 was pure cowpoke kitsch. This 6120 rests on a matching 1956 Gretsch Electromatic amp. Owner: Rikard Magnevill. (Photograph © *Vintage Guitar*)

It was the new medium of television that became the home for singing cowboys in this era, for the old westerns were logical inexpensive programming for stations cropping up all over the country. Not only did Gene and Roy and even Gabby Hayes have their own popular network series, but every major local station seemed to have a local singing cowboy—always with their horse and guitar close at hand—host a kids show that usually featured old westerns, often, unfortunately, brutally cut to fit television time format. If you grew up in the 1950s, you may remember Kenny Roberts in Saginaw and Dayton, Heck Harper in Portland, Fred Kirby in Charlotte, or Sheriff John in Los Angeles. They are just a handful of dozens who influenced a generation.

But western music and singing cowboys and their guitars basically lay fallow for two decades. Some still worked, of course: Rogers, the Sons of the Pioneers, Tex Ritter, Eddie Dean, and Jimmy Wakely continued to tour, but as the years went by they were viewed with nostalgia, a living symbol of simpler, gentler times.

It all came around again in the 1980s and 1990s, with the upstart success of Western revivalists Riders In The Sky and our successful television series' on The Nashville Network and CBS, and Michael Martin Murphey's bestselling pure cowboy albums, as well as the quirky success of several cowboy poetry gatherings, most notably the annual get together in Elko, Nevada. Western entertainers like Don Edwards, Gary McMahan, Ian Tyson, Red Steagall, and the Sons of the San Joaquin forged thriving careers, and a Western Music Association was formed to preserve and promote the songs and singers of the west, old and new. Today's singing cowboys, while no threat to Mariah Carey on the charts, occupy a significant niche in the American musical scene, highlighted by Riders in the Sky's appearance in Disney/Pixar's *Toy Story 2* and the subsequent Grammy award-winning album based on the movie, the first Grammy ever awarded to a Western group.

Yet through lean times and prosperous times, the image remains the same: The lone cowpoke or group of musical trail hands singing songs of the grandeur of the west or life on the trail, to the accompaniment of his faithful guitar . . . always his best friend besides his horse.

NAMING NAMES

"I used to play a place called Twist, Arkansas, on weekends, mostly at the beginning of my career. It got quite cold in Twist, so they would take a big garbage can, half-fill it with kerosene, and light that fuel for heat. One night in 1949 two guys got to fighting, and one of them knocked the other over on that container and it spilled on the floor. It looked like a river of fire. Everybody started running for the front door, including B.B. King. But when I got outside, I realized that I left my guitar, a Gibson acoustic, and I went back for it. When I did, the building started to collapse around me. I almost lost my life trying to save my guitar. The next morning we found out that the two guys had been fighting about a lady. I never did meet her, but I learned her name was Lucille. So I named my guitar—and every guitar I had since then—Lucille, to remind me never to do a thing like that again."
—B. B. King, *The B. B. King Companion*

B. B. KING AND HIS FAITHFUL LUCILLE

"This is my horse."
—Willie Nelson, on naming his Martin classical guitar "Trigger"

"Right after I'd seen Steve Winwood playing his white Strat, I was in Nashville and I went into this shop called Sho-Bud where they had stacks of Strats going for virtually nothing because they were so unfashionable and so unwanted. I bought a big pile of them all for a song—they were really cheap, like $300 or $400 each—and I took them home and gave them out. . . . I made Blackie out of a group of them: I took the pickups out of one, the scratchplate off another and the neck off another and I made my own guitar— a hybrid guitar that had all the best bits from all these Strats. . . . What makes Blackie unique for me is the fact that I made it! It was one of the last guitars that I actually built myself, really. Therefore it felt like it was invested with some kind of soul, you know."
—Eric Clapton

"She's a '59 stratocaster. I've always called her my First Wife. And she don't talk back to me, she talks for me. She don't scream at me, she screams for me."
—Stevie Ray Vaughan

The Twang Heard 'Round the World

The First Rock'n'Roll Guitar

By Michael Dregni

Michael Dregni is the veteran of several basement and garage bands with embarrassing names that played even more embarrassing music. He is the author of several obscure books on a variety of esoteric subjects, from Ferrari automobiles to motorscooters. He is a writer and reviewer for Vintage Guitar magazine, and at work on a biography of Django Reinhardt. A fan of "working class" guitars—National Duolians, single-pickup Fender Esquires, Gibson SJs, DiMauro Selmer-style copies—a Gibson ES-295 is the sole "gold" in his collection.

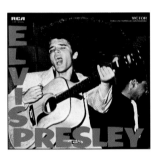  

It was the twang heard 'round the world.

Way back at the dawn of rock'n'roll history in July 1954, those first notes of Sun Records #209 came blasting out of your radio like a hound dog hit by lightning. The sound of Elvis Presley's supercharged hillbilly voice singing "That's All Right" was backed by Scotty Moore's twanging golden guitar. The world would never be the same.

Plucking his Gibson ES-295, Scotty's style was part country, part Travis picking, part something totally new. Whatever you called it, that twang reverberated far beyond the radio waves. Every aspiring rockabilly had to slow down Elvis' Sun Records to 16rpm and make those sounds. And many of them saved their pennies for an ES-295.

Scotty's choice of the golden guitar seemed just right to jumpstart a new music. In the early 1950s, men wore gray flannel suits, Betty Crocker was the homemaker's

1954 GIBSON ES-295

The ES-295 was Gibson's audacious golden-colored archtop with a rock'n'roll tone when the dials were turned up by Elvis's guitarman Scotty Moore. Built from 1952 through 1958, the 295 turned the world on to gold-colored guitars, a color scheme soon used on Gibson's Les Paul and offered as a custom color on Fender's Stratocaster. Owner: Michael Dregni.

heroine, and tailfins on cars were just a gleam in some mad designer's eyes; Gibson stood for big band jazz, Fender for country and western, and pedal steels were hot sellers. And then along came this audacious golden archtop at a time when guitars were only supposed to be *au naturel*—or painted with a funky "sunburst" if they didn't look good in their birthday suits. Whomever played a golden guitar was just asking for trouble. Gibson never planned it this way, but the ES-295 became the first rock'n'roll guitar, as outrageous as the music it stood for.

As with many things in the guitar universe, it was Les Paul who sparked the development of the ES-295. Back in 1951, Les asked Gibson to spray one of its stock ES-175 archtops in gold lacquer for an ailing vet who was a fellow fretter. Les tells the tale:

"Mary Ford and I were playing at Wood Hospital in Milwaukee in 1951 for injured war veterans. We would carry our guitars and amps from room to room. I was playing my Epiphone 'Clunker' and Mary sang.

"One vet named Dean Davis had his head all bandaged up from a brain tumor operation, and he was propped up so he could see us. He said, 'I am a guitar player but I'll never play again because I am paralyzed down one side of my body.'

"I said, 'It is possible to play with one hand,' and told him of my car accident and how I had my arm cast in plaster so I could still play.

"I asked him what song he wanted to hear and he picked a difficult one in the key of F#, 'Just One More Chance.' I turned my amp way up and I tapped out the chords with just one hand on the fretboard, and tears rolled down his face.

"I told him that I would have a guitar made for him, any kind he liked. He said he would like a golden archtop guitar.

"Out in the hallway, the doctor told me that the vet's case was terminal and he probably wouldn't last one week. I called Ted McCarty at Gibson immediately and said I needed a guitar right now—take an ES-175 and paint it gold. He said he would make it and ship it directly to the hospital. There was no publicity intended; it was just a gift.

"Well, the guitar arrived but the vet never saw it.

He died shortly after we visited him. His wife received the guitar and sent it back to me with a letter explaining of the vet's passing."

Les parked the golden ES-175 at his house for years until a friend borrowed it for just one night, during which it was lost in a nightclub fire. That guitar was serial number #A9196, registered on December 4, 1951. It was pure serendipity, but that spray-painted jazz-player's archtop became the prototype of the first rock'n'roll guitar.

Nothing more came of that sole one-off golden guitar, although subsequently at least two other ES-175s—serial numbers #A10137 and #A10474—were given the Midas touch in early 1952. Spraying a perfectly good 175 in gold paint was either sacrilegious or just downright silly, depending on your point of view. But then Les Paul liked things in the guitar world of the early 1950s that most people couldn't comprehend.

Still, a handful of golden ES-175s was not a production run. The true inspiration came once again from Les Paul's helping hand.

Throughout the late 1940s and early 1950s, Les

"THE LOG"
Les Paul created The Log in the 1940s to experiment with his advanced ideas for an electric solid body. To a solid chunk of 4x4 wood, he bolted a Larson Brother's neck with a Gibson headstock and two sides of an Epiphone body. It was weird, it was strange—and it was the future. Owner: Scott Chinery. (Photograph © *Vintage Guitar*)

had hounded Gibson to produce a solid-body electric guitar based on his own homebuilt "Log"—"the broomstick with the pickups on it," as he remembers CMI-Gibson president Maurice H. Berlin calling it. When Gibson finally changed its corporate mind and hustled to catch up with that upstart Leo Fender, Les remembers Berlin telling him that they would put his name on the solid body and build it to his specifications. Les again:

"M. H. asked me what I wanted, and I just spurted out 'gold!' as if I'd been rehearsing it. Well, if I'd had a bomb and thrown it, it couldn't have been any worse.

"The shop foreman stood up and said, 'That's the most god awful color you could pick!'

"And I said, '*Metallic* gold!' That was even worse.

"Berlin said, 'Hold it. Now Les, why do you want gold?'

"I said, 'Gold means rich. Gold means the best.'

"Berlin said, 'Gold it is.'"

And golden it was. The new Les Paul Model was officially added to the Gibson line in March 1952.

Following in the glare of the Les Paul, Gibson created an archtop version of its solid-body electric—or a golden version of its ES-175. Thus was born the ES-295, ES standing for Electric Spanish and the number designation denoting the price tag of $295. The first production ES-295s—serial numbers #A10554 and #A10555—were listed on May 14, 1952, some three months after the Les Paul debut.

The ES-295 was an ES-175 with the radical features of the Les Paul Model. It used the 16-inch laminated maple archtop body of the ES-175, the same nineteen-fret neck with double parallelogram inlays, and the 175's cutting-edge Florentine cutaway. But here the similarities ended.

Whereas the 175 was only available in 1952 with a single P-90 single-coil pickup, the 295 featured two, covered in ivory-colored Royalite to harmonize with the gold lacquer body and gold-plated parts. In a backflip of inspiration, the twin-pickup 295 would later prompt Gibson to create its double-pickup ES-175-D in 1954.

Like the Les Paul Model, the ES-295 featured Les' combination bridge–tailpiece, a long-reach tail with the bar bridge bolting directly to the guitar top. Les

Music, Sweet Music, Drips from My Fender's Fingers

Hendrix and Hardware

By Charles Shaar Murray

Jimi Hendrix is recognized as an undeniable genius of the electric guitar. Although he died in 1970 at the young age of twenty-seven—just three years after the release of his first album, Are You Experienced?*—he continues to be celebrated as one of history's most influential guitar players. In this excerpt from* Crosstown Traffic, *journalist Charles Shaar Murray demystifies the mechanics behind Hendrix's otherworldly guitar prowess. Charles is also the author of* Boogie Man: The Adventures of John Lee Hooker in the American Twentieth Century, *and his articles have appeared in magazines such as* Rolling Stone, The Face, *and* Vogue.

If the musicians of the sixties were, as Robert Wyatt says, "dragged along in the wake of their audiences' expectations," then the instrument manufacturers and recording engineers were, in turn, dragged along in the wake of the musicians' imaginations. Just as wars have traditionally been fought with strategies that proved successful in previous conflicts, so equally, each new stage in the evolution of the music was created with an older generation of technology. The earliest sound recordings served a purely documentary function as snapshots of "real" events; the electric guitar was initially considered as simply a louder version of its acoustic ancestor. A recording engineer's job was to get everything sounding as "realistic" as possible; a producer's—inasmuch as the term "producer" existed at the time—was to coax or bully the best performance he could from the musicians. Records were cut fast to reduce costs; Jerry Lee Lewis once boasted that "Whole Lotta Shakin' Goin' On" took "about as long to record as it does to listen to." The ten songs from The Beatles' first album which hadn't been previously released as

A GUITAR EXPERIENCE
Historic handbill for The Jimi Hendrix Experience's June 1967 stand at London's Saville Theatre.

singles were recorded in a single fourteen-hour session. When they played their legendary Shea Stadium show to an open-air audience of 55,000, The Beatles used less amplification than today's bands would bring into a good-sized club.

In the sixties, Phil Spector became recording's equivalent of a D. W. Griffith or a Cecil B. de Mille: he worked on a grand, Wagnerian scale, staging awesome spectacles—five guitarists, three drummers, platoons of strings—for his microphones, just as Griffith and DeMille did for their cameras. George Martin, spurred on by the drug-addled aural visions of The Beatles, put to work everything he had learned as the producer of The Goons' surreal comedy records, creating the extraordinary *trompe l'oreille* conjuring tricks of the fab moptops' later fantasias. Martin's production of The Beatles' records caught Jimi Hendrix's imagination as powerfully as Bob Dylan's lyrical virtuosity had done: like Martin, he saw the recording studio as an extension of his instrument, as a brush rather than a canvas.

Both as a guitarist and as a recording artist, Hendrix was following in the footsteps of Les Paul, a pivotal figure in the development of twentieth century music technology. Paul—born Lester Polfuss in 1916—was first and foremost a musician, and a very successful one, but his greatest impact was as an inventor. At nine, he "amplified" his acoustic guitar by stabbing the needle of his parents' gramophone into the instrument's vibrating wooden top; he pioneered multitrack recording and was building himself solid-body electric guitars in the early forties. The best-selling records he made with his wife Mary Ford were masterpieces of sound-on-sound collage, pasting together as many as twenty overdubs of guitar and voice, some speeded up or slowed down. His instrument designs were eventually adopted by Gibson—one of America's leading manufacturers—and their first mass-produced solid-body guitar still bears his name. (Initially, Gibson's executives were so dubious about the 'plank' guitar that their first instinct was to market the Les Paul without the company's logo.) If anybody is the missing link between Charlie Christian and Jimi Hendrix, it is Les Paul; he was the first person who really understood the extent to which the electric guitar was a new instrument, as different from the acoustic as a Hammond organ is from a Steinway piano—or a car from a horse.

Literally hundreds of companies have marketed electric guitars over the years; the best of them have produced instruments with distinct sounds and applications. The Beatles' records primarily showcased the rockabilly plunk of George Harrison's favored Gretsch instruments and the bright jangle of John Lennon's Rickenbackers, but from the early fifties onwards, electric guitar manufacturing in the USA was essentially dominated by Gibson and Fender, two companies utterly distinct in both their individual histories and their design philosophies. Gibson was established in the late nineteenth century by the brilliant, autocratic luthier Orville Gibson, and the expansion of the company and the evolution of its products was a stately but inexorable march of progress; technological innovation and traditional, conservative styling combined at every turn. The body of the Gibson Les Paul may have been a thick, carved chunk of prime solid mahogany, but it was also a miniature version of the company's pre-eminent line of premium jazz guitars. Like its big, hollow ancestors, its mahogany neck was firmly glued in place, and the crucial 24¾" "scale" length (the quantity of string between the bridge and the nut) remained.

Fender guitars were an entirely different sort of animal. Leo Fender certainly didn't invent the

1950s GIBSON LES PAUL STANDARD DUO

When guitarist Les Paul first showed up at Gibson's door with his solid-body electric guitar creation, he was shown right back out amid a chorus of chuckles. But soon after Leo Fender converted the world with his solid bodies, Gibson went looking for "that guy with the plank." The first of the Les Paul Model in 1952 featured two single-coils and a startling golden paint scheme. Humbuckers were added in 1957, as on this 1957 Goldtop, left. By 1958, stunning sunbursts showed off the Les Paul's figured tops, and the three years of the Les Paul 'Burst—1958, 1959, and 1960—make for some of the most coveted vintage guitars anywhere. Owners: Gil Southworth (Goldtop); Victor Lindenheim (Sunburst). (Photograph © *Vintage Guitar*)

solid body guitar—Les Paul had been there before him, as had Californian inventor Paul Bigsby and not a few others—but he was the instrument's Henry Ford; he was the one who figured out how to mass-produce and mass-market affordable solids. His first guitar, the Broadcaster—introduced in 1949 and renamed Telecaster two years later—was manufactured in modular form and then bolted and wired together; its neck was a single piece of rock maple with frets applied directly into the blond wood, its headstock was angled with all the tuners in one row to keep the strings straight for their entire length, and Fender's 25½" scale gave the Tele a higher string tension which complemented the high-frequency bias of his pick-ups. Leo Fender didn't even play the guitar himself; he was a former radio-repairman whose company had been founded on his amplifier line. The Telecaster was as untraditional as a guitar could get; no greater contrast with the plush opulence of the Gibson range could have been imagined.

Jimi Hendrix was a Fender man through and through. He experimented occasionally with Gibsons (his favorite being the spectacular Flying V . . .), but his instrument of choice was Fender's Stratocaster, unveiled in 1954. He owned more than a hundred of them over the years, very few of which are known to have survived. (Buddy Miles, Monika Danneman, Al Kooper, Frank Zappa and Mitch Mitchell owned authenticated Hendrix Strats; Billy Gibbons of ZZ Top has one of slightly less impeccable pedigree.) To this day, UK instrument dealers refer to Stratocasters made between 1966 and 1971 (or reissues thereof) as "Hendrix Strats."

Leo Fender and his crew designed the Stratocaster as a more elegant and elaborate development of the plain, workman-like Telecaster. The Telecaster's body was a flat plank; the Stratocaster's was contoured at the back to fit around the player's ribcage and tapered at the front to accommodate the right forearm. Where the Telecaster mimicked the single cutaway of previous electric guitars, the Stratocaster's body was cut away above and below the neck, like horns. The Telecaster had two pickups—one at the butt of the neck and the other just above the bridge—to the Stratocaster's

three. Fender had originally intended the Strat's pick-ups to be heard separately, since he didn't like the sound they made when combined; however, guitarists disagreed, and soon discovered that by carefully lodging the pick-ups' selector switch between the designated positions, two further sounds were available. (In the early seventies, spare-parts companies began to manufacture five-way switches for installation in Stratocasters; a few years later, Fender conceded and began supplying Strats with five-ways as a standard feature.)

Unlike Gibson's guitars—and, for that matter, the Telecaster—the Strat's volume and tone controls were placed close to the bridge, so that the player could manipulate them without having to interrupt the music by reaching down. Gibson, still thinking of the electric as a different sort of acoustic guitar, presumably worked on the principle that a player would carefully adjust the sound to suit his or her requirements, and then concentrate on playing. The Stratocaster's design assumed that the guitarist might conceivably want to modify tone, volume and pick-up selection *while playing.*

Finally, the Strat came equipped with the most elegant and reliable handvibrato system then available; a thin metal bar which protruded from the bridge and raised or lowered the tension (and therefore the pitch) of the strings. Most of the musicians Fender knew played country music, and the Strat's accessible volume control and hand vibrato (generally, and inaccurately, referred to as a 'tremolo') enabled a guitarist to mimic the swells and bends of the pedal steel guitar. What Fender had in mind when he designed the Strat tremolo, though, was something far more genteel than the pedalto-the-metal savagery Hendrix inflicted upon it; it is therefore not so surprising that on many of his live recordings Hendrix was so frequently out of tune. The tremolo system simply wasn't up to it (neither, for that matter, were the guitar strings available at the time), and guitarists unwilling to undertake drastic retuning between—or even during—tunes generally fought shy of using tremolos until more stable, lockable versions were introduced in the early eighties by the Floyd Rose and Kahler companies.

The Stratocaster had been a favorite of some of the radical blues guitarists of the fifties—Buddy Guy, Ike Turner, Otis Rush, Pee Wee Crayton and others had found it eminently suitable for their needs—but until the arrival of Jimi Hendrix, it was most commonly associated (in the USA) with Buddy Holly and (in the UK) with Hank B. Marvin of The Shadows. Both of them were gifted, inventive guitarists who loved the Stratocaster for its clean-cut tones, versatility and general ease of handling, but as far as the new blues-rock hotshots were concerned, it was a guitar for skinny, bespectacled nerds. The most prized snob guitar to own in 1966 was the Gibson Les Paul, both because its thick, rich sound (jointly attributable to its body construction and to the double-coil "humbucking" pick-ups Gibson had used since 1958) lent itself to the new vogue for overdriven, distorted sustain, and also because Gibson had discontinued the Les Paul line in 1960, due to a combination of declining sales and various disputes with Les Paul himself. All the trendsetting guitarists—Eric Clapton, Jeff Beck, Peter Green, Michael Bloomfield—used them, and you had to be a pretty cool dude even to *have* one, let alone know what to do with it.

During his chitlin circuit years, Hendrix had used whatever guitars he could afford; Fender Jazzmasters and Duo-Sonics, Epiphone Coronets and Wilshires and assorted others. He had had to pawn or sell too many guitars in times of economic hardship to get too hung up on any one instrument, but the Stratocaster had been his preference ever since his days with the Isley Brothers. Though he was left-handed, he had grown accustomed to conventional, right-handed models which he would then restring and modify to suit his particular requirements; he removed the nut, replacing it upside-down, and readjusted the string height and intonation at the bridge. Unlike Bobby Womack, Otis Rush, Albert King and Defunkt's Ronnie Drayton, he chose to retain conventional chord and scale constructions rather than create new patterns to play on a right-hand-strung guitar, and he seldom bothered with special left-hand models, both because right-handed guitars were more plentiful and easier to obtain, and because—with a touchingly

American faith in mass-production—he believed that they were likely to be manufactured to a higher standard. The double cutaway allowed him to reach almost all the top frets, especially since he had exceptionally long fingers.

Inevitably, his modifications gave the instrument a slightly different sound. The pick-ups were set to provide what Fender considered optimum response from each string, but of course, Hendrix's reverse-stringing meant that the strings weren't in the positions they were supposed to occupy. Furthermore, the bridge pick-up was angled so that it "heard" the treble strings closer to the bridge than the basses; for Hendrix the reverse was true. The single-sided headstock was designed so that the string tension was heaviest on the bass E and lightest on the treble E, but again, for Hendrix it worked the opposite way. The results he achieved with his jury-rigged set-up were so spectacular that right-handed guitarists—Steve Miller is one example—began buying left-handed Stratocasters and having them strung and set up right-handed. "Reverse staggered" pick-ups can be bought from various accessory companies; Stevie Ray Vaughan has one of his Stratocasters fitted with a left-hand tremolo system, and reverse headstocks are currently intensely fashionable. All these devices are supposed to bring the guitarist a silly millimeter nearer to Hendrix's own sound.

The Stratocaster didn't lend itself to distortion with anywhere near the ease of the Les Paul, but Hendrix turned this, too, to his advantage. The unmodified Fender sound has a clean, sharp high-frequency response which the Gibson cannot match, but the various distortion-inducing floor-pedals he used—"fuzz-box" was the generic term of the era—could garbage up his sound until it matched anything a Gibson could produce. End result: an unparalleled palette of guitar sounds unavailable elsewhere.

Second only in importance to Hendrix's Stratocaster was his acquisition—almost immediately after arrival in Britain—of the brand-new Marshall 100-watt "stack." It was the creation of Jim Marshall, a former big-band drummer and drum tutor (Mitch Mitchell was among his pupils) who had opened a

CUSTOM-COLOR FENDER STRATOCASTER TRIO
The stock sunburst finish of the Stratocaster was a rather staid style for such a wildly futuristic guitar. Many owners paid the extra cost for a custom paint job and finally had curves with color to match. From left, a 1965 Burgundy Mist; 1958 blonde Mary Kaye with gold hardware; and a 1965 Inca Silver. Owner: Ron De Marino. (Photograph © *Vintage Guitar*)

hugely successful instrument shop in Ealing. As musicians demanded more power and volume than could be delivered by the exceedingly rare and expensive Fender amplifiers or by Vox, the leading domestic brand beloved of The Shadows, The Beatles and their admirers, Marshall grew sick of having to repair them, and—egged on by Eric Clapton and The Who—set about building something sturdier. Once Marshall had developed the 100-watt head, Pete Townshend insisted on a monster cabinet containing eight 12" speakers, but faced with a potential roadies' strike, he settled for the more manageable arrangement of two stackable cabinets containing four speakers each. This rapidly became the industry standard it remains today, and the "wall of Marshalls" was institutionalized as a trademark of the Second British Invasion. (Townshend is still vaguely niggled that Hendrix carted his Marshalls to the Monterey Pop Festival while The Who had to make do with rented Fenders; not only did these amps not produce the sound to which The Who were accustomed, but they weren't allowed to smash them for their grand finale.)

Marshalls weren't just louder than anything that had come before, they were also more sensitive; their preamps sucked up more of the sound of the guitar's pick-ups than Fenders or Voxes. For Hendrix, this meant that the guitar was, literally, "alive" all over; he could produce sounds by lightly tapping the instrument's neck or body (or, of course, by banging them as hard as he could), generating his unique onomatopoeic guitar language without playing an actual note. At high volumes, the impacts would jar the guitar into feedback (the sound of the amplifier's speakers reintroduced into the pick-ups, instantly transformed into a hum or a scream), creating tones which sounded more like a synthesizer than a guitar. The resulting pitch could then be raised or lowered with the tremolo, giving Hendrix access to sounds unobtainable by anybody else before the introduction of affordable synthesizer technology. (As an example, the multi-overdubbed studio version of "The Star Spangled Banner" issued on the posthumous *Rainbow Bridge* is pure "synthesizer"—although it was actually created with a multiplicity of feedback guitars and basses further modified with variable tape-speed.)

Habitually, Hendrix would run his Marshalls with all tone and volume controls turned full up to 10, adjusting the levels directly from the guitar. From years of experience, he would be able to position his body and his guitar relative to the amplifier's speaker cabinets so that the resulting feedback would modulate to the precise tone he wanted: a high harmonic, a low fundamental or a tone transitional between the two. For crash-and-burn extravaganzas like the climax of "Machine Gun" or the intro to the Monterey version of "Wild Thing," he would summon up a raw explosion of sound by clouting the guitar, "select" the required frequency by moving back and forth until it emerged from the *mêlée*, move it up or down by raising or lowering the tremolo arm, and "interrupt" it or make it "flutter" by interposing his body between the guitar's pick-ups and the amplifier's speakers. When he wanted to return to conventional playing, he could do so by turning the guitar's volume down to manageable levels, and then moving out of feedback range.

As soon as he got the money to indulge himself, Hendrix rapidly became an ardent technophile. He ran up colossal bills at prestigious New York music shops, buying every new gadget as it came on the market; his Electric Lady recording studio was designed to be the most modern, the most luxurious and the best-equipped in the world. That his work as both a recording and performing musician now seems like a shining testament to what can be achieved with "old" or "low" technology is simply a manifestation of historical irony; he used the most advanced stuff he could lay his hands on at the time, from the custom floor-pedals like the Octavia and the Univibe which he commissioned from Roger Mayer, to be the then-futuristic gadgetry he installed at Electric Lady. Hendrix would not only have been utterly at home in the contemporary world of Synclaviers, Fairlights and Apple Macintosh music

HAIL THE KING!
Jimi Hendrix always acknowledged his debt to the bluesmen and R&B bands that came before him. And in turn, even B. B. King paid homage to Jimi's guitarwork.

PLEASURE PIER
MARINE ROOM
GALVESTON, TEXAS
WEDNESDAY, JULY 20
9 P. M. UNTIL
ADMISSION PRE SALE $1.50
AT DOOR $1.75
IN PERSON
B.B. KING
AND HIS Sensational 10 PIECE BAND
AMERICAN PRINTING & LITHOGRAPHING CO.—DALLAS

software, but he would probably—if he had survived—have been among the first to adopt them as basic, workaday tools.

Alan Douglas, who supervised many of Hendrix's later recording sessions, has said that no one could produce Hendrix's records; all a producer could do was to help him produce himself. Though this may well have been true by 1969—when they first started to record together—the statement seems more like a dig at Chas Chandler than an objective assessment of Hendrix's recording career. As a producer, Hendrix's forte was the creation of weird and wonderful new sounds and effects; the more orthodox and mundane task of recording straight, basic instrumental sounds probably seemed a trivial one to him. *Electric Ladyland* (1968) was the first album on which he assumed production credits (even though a few of the songs had been recorded the previous year under the Chandler administration), and it admirably highlights this dichotomy. The bass and drums on—for example—"Voodoo Chile (Slight Return)" are, even on CD, appallingly muzzy and indistinct; not a patch on the clear, punchy rhythm tracks on George Martin's Beatles records, the Stax soul hits or even his own early Experience records, all of which were recorded on far more primitive gear than that used on *Ladyland*. More than a few of his later records—many of which were, admittedly, mixed and completed by others after his death—are chaotic and disorienting, with eccentric balance levels and stereo imaging. By contrast, his near-contemporary and fellow guitarist-producer Jimmy Page built his multi-platinum-selling Led Zeppelin records on thunderously tight and clear bass and drum foundations, "professionalizing" hard-rock recording just as the megawatt P.A. systems the group used for their live performances "professionalized" stadium rock shows. Again, the deluge of live Hendrix recordings issued in the last couple of decades demonstrates clearly how his voice—hardly the sturdiest vocal instrument at the best of times—suffered for the lack of effective stage monitoring, when the awesomely concussive levels of amplification he used rendered it almost impossible for him to hear what he was singing. (His tendency to forget lyrics on stage didn't help, it must be admitted.)

Nevertheless, *Electric Ladyland*'s two longest pieces—"Voodoo Chile" on side one and "1983/A Merman I Should Turn to Be" on side three—effectively demonstrate the extremes of his approach as a producer/musician. "Voodoo Chile" is a jam: a straight extension of venerable Delta blues themes performed more or less spontaneously by Hendrix with Mitch Mitchell on drums, Jefferson Airplane's Jack Casady on bass and Stevie Winwood behind the organ. Here we find Hendrix wrestling with wood and wires, creating on his feet in a form where inspiration is all. (A blues jam without genuine feeling or a constant flow of ideas achieves levels of tedium unknown outside double-glazing sales conferences.) Recorded "live in the studio," it is "hand-son" music-making of the most traditional, lo-tech variety, a lengthy four-way conversation which was probably utterly unrepeatable. "1983," by contrast, is a lengthy studio fantasia which collages a variety of performances; embellished with sound effects and constructed on tape in a manner as unreproducible in live performance as The Beatles' *Sgt Pepper* was at the time. The final "performance" was not by the band; it was by Hendrix and his engineer Eddie Kramer, and the "instrument" was a mixing desk. There is nothing like it anywhere else in pop; it steers a supremely sure-footed path between the fumbling abstractions of contemporary Pink Floyd records and the art-deco cartooning of The Beatles. It is rock's premier work of science fiction; Hendrix was the music's first and funkiest cyberpunk.

As a guitarist, he remains imitated but unassimilated; Eddie Van Halen, by far the most influential hard and heavy guitarist of the eighties, has borrowed the Hendrix vocabulary—tremolo tricks and all—in order to say very little, while defiantly citing

1968 GIBSON FLYING V

The Flying V might have been too outrageous for the 1950s, but by the 1960s it seemed perfect for the new era of rock'n'roll excess. Gibson relaunched the Flying V in 1966 with new appointments. This 1968 V leans against a 1965 Vox Super Reverb Twin. Owner: Craig Brody. (Photograph © *Vintage Guitar*)

Eric Clapton (whom he resembled about as much as I do Tom Cruise) as his primary influence. Prince, with equal perversity, names Carlos Santana as his guitar guru, even as he unleashes patently Hendrix-derived flourishes as both theatrical device and sound effect—though he has gone on record as suggesting that mastering "The Star Spangled Banner" is an essential rite of passage for any tyro electric guitarist. Meanwhile, Hendrix fetishism continues unabated among the guitar fraternity: the most valuable recent contributions to Hendrixology come from magazines like *Guitar Player* and *Guitar World* . . . and he appears, from the grave, to endorse as many products as most living guitar stars.

The "Hendrix Strats" advertised by UK Fender dealers represent unofficial collectors' shorthand rather than an authorized signature model like Fender's Eric Clapton and Yngwie Malmsteen Stratocasters, but Hendrix's name and image do appear on Jim Dunlop's special-edition reissues of the old Dallas-Arbiter Fuzz Face distortion box and Vox Cry Baby wah-wah pedal he favored. I bought a "Jimi Hendrix" wah-wah (Model JH-1)—purely in the interests of research, of course—and found, on its base, a logo depicting a silhouette of Hendrix, a discography of recommended albums (including the posthumous cut-and-paste *Crash Landing*, which does not often figure in such lists), and a stern warning to the effect that "any use of the Jimi Hendrix name with effects pedals without the consent of the Hendrix Estate Management and Dunlop Mfg Co is prohibited by law."

There's nothing wrong with all of this—after all, Hendrix did use these particular gizmos, and the reissues are made to the exact specifications of the originals—but the most specious "posthumous endorsement" came in 1985, when Schecter, the U.S. guitar and accessory company, announced their Jimi Hendrix Model, a right-handed Strat clone with a left-handed neck and "Jimi Hendrix Signature Model" reverse-staggered pick-ups, complete with a scrawled "Jimi Hendrix" on the scratchplate, though it was not a facsimile of Hendrix's actual signature. Duran Duran's guitarist Andy Taylor appeared in the company's ads

1966 FENDER JAGUAR
Introduced in 1962, Fender's Jaguar was a gearhead's delight, designed to entice guitarists with its array of rocker switches, two single-coil pickups, whammy bar, and its most bizarre feature, a spring-loaded string mute. Few players actually wanted to mute their strings, but the Jaguar won a legion of fans turned on by the guitar's over-the-top gadgetry. Owner: Chris Matthes. (Photograph © *Vintage Guitar*)

under the legend, "Hendrix has inspired a whole generation of guitarists. Now he's inspired a guitar." The ad presumably inspired a terse communication from the Hendrix estate's lawyers: the Jimi Hendrix Model rapidly disappeared from Schecter's catalogue, to be replaced by an instrument known as the H Series, identical in all respects except for the absence of the "signature." Hendrix's next endorsement is keenly awaited by guitarists everywhere.

WHY I PLAY GUITAR

"There's a lot in this hair of mine that I've got to get out."
—Jimi Hendrix

"I wanted to definitely be a musician or a good preacher or a heck of a baseball player. I couldn't play ball too good—I hurt my finger and I stopped that. I couldn't preach, and well, all I had left was getting into the music thing."
—Muddy Waters, quoted in Robert Gordon's *Can't Be Satisfied: The Life and Times of Muddy Waters*

"It just happened. I felt it. I couldn't stop thinking about it. All of a sudden I wanted a guitar, and that was it."
—Neil Young, *The Rolling Stone Interviews: 1967–1980*

"I'm not a champion of the guitar as an instrument. The guitar is just one of the most compact and sturdy. And the reason I still play is that the more you do, the more you learn. I found a new chord the other day. I was like, 'Shit, if I had know that years ago....' That's what's beautiful about the guitar. You think you know it all, but it keeps opening up new doors. I look at life as six strings and twelve frets. If I can't figure out everything that's in there, what chance do I have of figuring out anything else?"
—Keith Richards *Rolling Stone* magazine

"Initially, there's that feeling of potential, of power, when you strap on an electric guitar. And then you learn that what it's really about is controlling that power. I mean, the guitar has been a big part of rock & roll. I just can't imagine Elvis holding a violin!"
—The Edge, *The Rolling Stone Interviews: The 1980s*

"I think acoustic guitars are incredible, because you can write a song on one and take it anywhere you want."
—Beth Orton, *Guitar Player* magazine

"What I love most about the guitar is there are no rules. You make them up as you go along."
—Steve Howe, *Guitar Player* magazine

"If pianos were lighter, maybe I'd play one."
—Dave Matthews

COWBOY GUITAR STAR WANNABE
Everyone with a guitar dreamed of being a hand at Melody Ranch.

CHAPTER 3

Rebel with a Guitar

POWER CHORD
A lounge guitarist hits a power chord on his dot-neck Gibson
ES-335 TD and dreams of the big time.

The Idiot's Hammer
A Punk Manifesto
By Scott Puckett

Sometimes the guitar doesn't need to be deftly played to be a thing of beauty. Scott Puckett, a writer, roadie, and all-around music fan, has tried to play more instruments than Police Academy has sequels and failed at all of them. These days, Scott muses about the nature of musicianship in an amateur world of self-recording and ponders buying a four-track to make his numerous musical shortcomings that much more apparent. Here, he introduces us to the guitar from a punk's-eye view.

The first guitar I ever had was a beat-up $100 six-string acoustic pawn shop special. And, to be completely truthful, it wasn't mine. My dad (who later turned out not to be my dad, but that's another story) had bought it in the mid-80's so that he could accompany his school's choir. He bought chord books and everything—even went to a couple of lessons. Learning how to play an instrument turned out to be something that pretty closely resembled actual *work* though, so the idea of adding instrumentation to the kids' voices fell by the wayside. And so too did the guitar.

ROYAL FLUSH
Inset: Just fifty examples of the Royal Flush were made in Japan in the 1980s. Owner: Dennis Fleischauer.

GUITAR MONSTER
Opposite page: Herman Munster was Dr. Frankenstein's second attempt at creating a monster—and again things went horribly wrong. On TV's *The Munsters*, Herman cruised town in The Munstermobile and strummed a guitar. And although he tried hard to be an upstanding citizen, his wife Lily fretted that his irresistible good looks would tempt other women. All part of the life of a guitar monster!

He didn't really notice when the case migrated from his study to my bedroom, or maybe he did and was just relieved that my mom wouldn't be asking him about it anymore. "Honey, why don't you practice guitar anymore? You spent $100 on it. It's a shame to see it go to waste." "Oh, the boy's playing around with it. I figure I'll let him have his fun and when he gets bored, he won't notice when I take it away." I could imagine them having that discussion; hell, I could practically *hear* it.

There was only one problem.

I didn't get bored.

And that acoustic guitar stayed in my room until I moved out.

At this point, I should note that I am not a guitar player by trade, training or talent. I have never played guitar professionally in my life. I have been fortunate enough to have the good sense not to tape anything I've played. I am, all things considered, a horrible guitar player. I have no skill and no discernible aptitude for learning how to play what my friend Pierre calls the Idiot's Hammer.

I should also note that I am a punk. I have a deep and abiding affection for punk rock. I listen to music that requires—at its most basic level—no more than three chords and I couldn't even manage *that*. I couldn't even play a proper power chord without hitting the wrong string.

But that beat-to-hell acoustic guitar stayed in my room anyway. It was a good friend for a lot of late nights, even after it went out of tune. Even after I broke strings. Even after I took a cue from Sonic Youth and started beating on it with drumsticks to see what other, perhaps more interesting, sounds I could wrench from its hollow body. That cheap pawn shop guitar saw me through some of the hardest times I would ever know, even though my awkward, fumbling fingers could never give voice to the music I heard in my head.

I haven't seen that guitar in years. But I still regret what I did to it.

I got my second guitar about a week after my mother killed herself. It was a Fender Squier Strat. I bought it at a guitar store that no longer exists. My friend Philip went with me and I still laugh about his rules.

"If you look at anything besides Fender or Gibson, I'll kick your ass," he said.

"What about a Rickenbacker?" I asked.

He thought for a moment and said, "Okay. I won't kick your ass for looking at a Rickenbacker, but you won't be able to afford one yet."

He was right.

And I walked out of the store with my Fender. Black on black. No inlays on the fretboard. Nothing fancy. Not even a *case*. Just a black guitar, six strings and the blues. I drank a lot of gin and bourbon that month and I played every day until my fingers bled. I still couldn't hit a power chord, but my drunken, fumbling, bloody fingers managed to pick out a few nice guitar lines here and there.

I've been playing that guitar for years now. I can't even count how many sets of strings I've gone through, how many nights I've spent smoking while I struggled through Replacements and Lou Reed songs, how many times I'd play some rudimentary progression for a friend and hand my guitar over to them, only to hear them articulate what I could only hear and hum; only to find that my guitar, like some of my former lovers, was more responsive in another man's hands.

But I love that fickle bitch anyway.

Finally, I came to my senses and switched to bass. As I told people at the time, I started playing music as a drummer. I picked up the guitar because I loved bands like Hüsker Dü, because I could hear what musicians like Richard Thompson played and I wanted to see what I could do. Bass offered two fewer strings— two fewer chances for me to fuck up. Besides, I could

1966 RICKENBACKER MODEL 360
Rickenbacker was always on the avant garde of guitardom. From its pioneering Frying Pan electrics to the radical curves of its Capri, Ricks were far from ordinary. The glorious semi-hollow Model 360 with its slash fretmarkers and soundhole became Rickenbacker's trademark, an idiosyncratic guitar with flashy style and a sonic sensibility to match. The Jetglo Model 370 dates from 1968. Owner: Craig Brody/Guitar Broker. (Photograph ©Vintage Guitar)

1932 NATIONAL DUOLIAN

In the days before electrical pickups and amplification, Czech immigrant John Dopyera's National metal-bodied guitars with their aluminum resonating cones were an eccentric and innovative invention. And even when electric guitars surpassed the Nationals and spinoff Dobro firm's wares in loudness, inexpensive single-cone guitars such as this Duolian continued to offer greater volume down on the farm where rural electrification had yet to stretch its lines. Thus, the National was long the guitar of choice for Mississippi Delta bluesmen. Owner: Michael Dregni.

slow down. I loved how Greg Norton and Peter Hook and John Entwhistle's bass lines sounded.

Two P basses and no lessons later, I bought a Dobro.

And that's not exactly accurate either. Gibson owns the trademark for Dobro. In case you aren't familiar with what a Dobro is, it's a resonating guitar. In short, there's a metal cone, usually aluminum, set in the body of an otherwise hollow guitar body. The cone amplifies the notes; it also provides a highly distinct sound—a little tinny, a bit of echo . . . playing one is almost like stepping into an old blue session. John Dopyera invented resonators in the 1920s. He started a company called National (which provided a home for Adolph Rickenbacker—name sound familiar?—around the same time Dopyera departed) and left to develop DOBRO—a combination of Dopyera Brothers—guitars. Litigation resulted in a merger—time passed, the company changed names and finally Gibson bought it.

All this is a roundabout way of saying that I own a National-style resonating guitar. Not a Dobro. If you ever want to see a guitar so beautiful that it will literally take your breath away, take a look at one of the Gibson Dobros. Me? I doubt I'll ever play well enough to deserve an instrument like that.

I love my resonator though. I picked up glass and steel slides for it, figuring—perhaps correctly—that if I focused on notes and single strings, I could eventually learn the fretboard well enough to be a passable blues player or maybe pick up some decent lap steel skills. And so far, that hasn't happened either. I just keep picking out the same Replacements and Lou Reed songs, trying to puzzle out Bob Mould and Richard Thompson leads, and looking for tablature with chord diagrams.

I am, after all, a punk at heart. And impatient.

I don't want to learn music theory.

I simply want to play.

With anyone. Anywhere. Any style. For any reason.

With that said, my resonator, much as I love it, is in pieces at the moment. During one of my many moves, part of the biscuit bridge fell out. I contacted a local store here that also performs small guitar

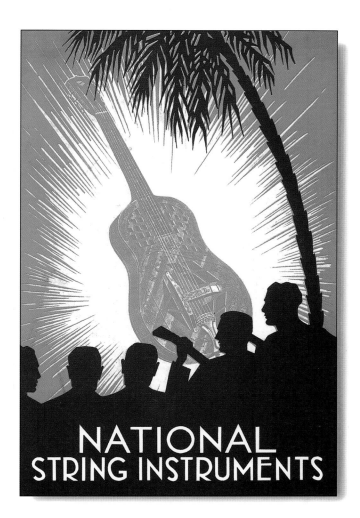

repairs—the owner told me to bring the guitar by. And in 60 minutes, I learned more about my guitar in his shop that I had ever known about any instrument. He deftly disassembled it, took the face plate off and saw what was wrong. He didn't have a biscuit bridge but he went into the back of the shop and rattled around for a bit and came back out with a piece of plastic and a small saw. He measured the bridge, marked the plastic and cut it to fit. Then I went to the hobby shop next door and bought a slender piece of balsa wood and cut it down to size.

I spent the next week sanding, filing and cutting a custom part for my resonator. No clamps. Just my hands and a table. No gloves. I have more than a few scabs on my fingers and knuckles right now and the piece still isn't done but I'm working with my hands, making something, fixing something that isn't a computer, for one of the first times in my life.

And it feels damn satisfying.

Yeah, I know I can probably buy a biscuit bridge, but fighting to make one from scratch, the way guitar players used to do it, holds a certain appeal for me. I feel more connected with the guitar, even though I still can't play it for shit. Fashioning the part with a knife and some wood seems more . . . authentic. It seems more honest. It seems *true*.

With all that said, guitar is still an easy instrument to play badly—particularly when it comes to punk rock —and I manage to do that well. My fingers stutter on the strings and they can't speak the words I need to say in the language I need to hear. I can't manage the three chords; I can't even manage one chord that I can identify or regularly play. By all rights, I should have given up by now because I'm really no good at it and show no signs of getting better.

But then I listen to Woody Guthrie's picking. It sounds simple, like anyone can do it. And that's part of what punk was about, right? Breaking down the barriers between the amateur and the professional, bringing music back to the people. It was music played by people who frequently couldn't play music, and since I can't play music, in some weird way that means that I'm making music, right? That draws a direct line from Woody Guthrie and Robert Johnson through Gene Vincent and Eddie Cochran to Joe Strummer and the Raincoats . . . to me.

I was talking with my buddy Davey about this once. I hop in the van with his band on occasion. I'm sort of a roadie, but mostly I just drive and smoke a lot and periodically haul amps around. He's actually the one who inspired me to get a resonator. I was telling him how much I love playing guitar even though I have no idea of what I'm doing, rambling on in that self-deprecating vein until he stopped me and said, "It's more like you don't know what you're doing right."

He's right. I don't. But sometimes, I can hear it. And on those nights, I go to bed around dawn with bloody fingers and I sleep a very satisfied sleep indeed.

I'm a punk. And I'm a lousy guitar player. But I am a guitar aficionado in the true spirit of that word. It takes dedication to continue to fail at something for so long. But in my eyes, the only thing I'm doing is failing to quit doing something I love.

And I do love my guitars.

HILLBILLY PUNKS
Above: The Smokey Oaks Trio pushes the boundaries of respectability. Whatever would come next?

1960s GIBSON SG DUO
Opposite page: With slumping sales of the Les Paul Standard, Gibson redesigned its leading solid-body electric with dual cutaways and a thinner body, all no doubt influenced by the best-selling Stratocaster. The new SG was unveiled in 1960 but only lasted until 1965 when the model was retired. The custom-color green SG Standard with long-body Vibrola was built in 1965. The cherry red SG Les Paul with sideways Vibrola dates to 1961. Owner: Jim Singleton. (Photograph © *Vintage Guitar*)

How to Smash and Burn a Guitar

By Eric Dregni

Eric Dregni is the guitar god of the baroque punk band Vinnie & The Stardüsters. Among the band's albums are The Baroque Wind Sessions *and* Novelty Music for Casual Sex, *which won an esteemed "Explicit Lyrics" note from amazon.com. He proudly plays a Korean Strat copy sacreligiously retrofitted with humbucker pickups through a Fender tweed 4x10 Bassman (reissue) and a motley assortment of stompboxes—including a super-special-cool Soviet-made Big Muff—on permanent loan from his brother. He prefers cheap lightweight orange no-name picks.*

A guitar god changed my life.

I was fourteen and The Who had come to town. It was my first concert and their first—but far from last—"Farewell Tour." They played the St. Paul Civic Center, and I witnessed the brilliance of Pete Townshend as he demonstrated how to properly wail on a guitar. Perhaps my judgment was skewed when scary-looking men in the bathroom pushed tiny pieces of paper imprinted with cartoon characters on me and I began hyperventilating the clouds of strange-smelling smoke emanating from the stalls.

In any case, I saw the light.

Towards the end of the three-and-a-half-hour-long concert, Roger Daltrey swung his microphone around his head to rouse the crowd. This bit of tomfoolery only provoked a few yawns. Yet the possibility that Townshend might smash his guitar into a hundred pieces brought everyone in the arena to their feet. We raised our Bic lighters high in reverence to our idol. Before the tour began, Townshend had vowed not to destroy any

SMASHED GUITAR
Bob Stinson of The Replacements demolished this Hamer at an outdoor May 1984 show at Grinnell College, Iowa. Stinson said he smashed the guitar because the band was pissed off that they had to warm up for The Wallets. It's as good a reason as any. Owner: Leif Larsen. (Photograph © Eric Dregni)

more instruments, but during the encore he couldn't resist bouncing his Stratocaster off the stage a couple times. He picked it up and gave it a few more whacks on the ground for good measure. It wasn't completely smashed but it was close enough for rock'n'roll. The crowd went wild.

The next day, I gave up piano lessons. The guitar was my calling. Besides, the piano brings visions of Liberace—even the antics of Jerry Lee Lewis playing with his feet could barely prove that the piano is a rock instrument. No more Chopin preludes or Gershwin show tunes for me. Pianos are made for rock stars to push into swimming pools in rebellion against classical music, or perhaps just plain, aimless rebellion. Smashing a piano would require far too much effort, not to mention a sharp axe and the possibility of losing an eye from all those high-tension piano strings snapping at me with each chop. The time it would take to destroy a piano would send any audience to the Land of Nod. I was ready for three-chord rock anthems, screaming guitar solos followed by a fit of rage in which I'd smash my guitar into a million pieces. It was a higher calling.

I researched the art of smashing a guitar. I did a little outside reading on the subject and studied as never before. Here's what I learned.

For maximum effect, avoid popping the body off from the neck in the first couple of swings if you want more than a three-second show. Start by spearing your amp, and don't hold back on the thrusts out of fear of electrocution. Wouldn't that only add to the legendary performance if you were hauled out on a stretcher? Swing at the drummer's crash cymbals, and hopefully the drummer will trash his set too. Splinters from the shattered wood should fly dangerously into the crowd as collector's items for those who dare risk being impaled. Most importantly, keep the ear-wrenching feedback screaming, otherwise any rock'n'roll furor will seem like a silent temper tantrum. At the end, leave the stage immediately without looking back.

Be creative in demolishing your instruments. Everyone knows the tale of Jimi Hendrix dousing his Strat in lighter fluid and setting it aflame at the 1967 Monterey Pop Festival while poor upstaged Pete Townshend fumed that he couldn't skewer his amp with his guitar because the amp was a rental. For a

teenager like myself, I was dazzled by this brilliant combination of the best of both worlds in Jimi's artistry—destruction *and* pyromania. Ace Frehley of Kiss crafted a built-in box under his Gibson Les Paul Custom's rhythm pickup to stuff with smoke bombs, then wore an asbestos-fronted costume so he wouldn't get burned. I worshipped him like the Thomas Edison of guitar pyrotechnics.

Now, I needed a guitar to smash. My friends were hesitant to lend me their Ovation guitars, even when I insisted I'd be doing them a favor. Instead, I went into the woods and practiced smashing oak branches, which is not as easy as may seem. I eventually took up Jimi's technique and set them afire. Even when I'd splash kerosene on my ersatz guitar for a fireball finale in the best Kiss tradition, my friends still didn't understand that I was a rock'n'roll god in training and not just some pyromaniacal cub scout.

With the arrival of New Wave, however, guitar smashing was suddenly passé. Hairdos and electric drums stole the limelight from gratuitous guitar solos. After all, who could imagine Duran Duran trashing a Roland synthesizer and battering all that circuitry?

Luckily, punk burst on the scene. The Clash plastered a silhouette of guitar smashing on the cover of *London Calling* as an effigy to the most sacred of all rock'n'roll acts. Sid Vicious of the Sex Pistols wielded his bass as a weapon to keep angry fans off the stage during a tour of Texas. Rock'n'roll was saved, and I found new idols I could truly admire.

I finally conned a friend into lending me his cheap electric guitar, but now I needed a band as a background for my screaming solos—even though I only knew three chords. I found a punk drummer from a Boston band called Expando Brain and a church youth-group pal who had no reservations about spouting out the most impressive list of profanity I'd ever heard. Inspired by a falling-down drunk named Vinnie that we met at the Stardust Bowling Alley who tried to sell us drugs, we named ourselves Vinnie & The Stardüsters. (The umlaut was strictly for effect and not pronunciation.)

Our rock'n'roll heroes were Minneapolis' hometown heroes, The Replacements, who kept the guitar-smashing tradition alive at their liquor-fueled concerts.

BARBECUE PARTY
All the ingredients needed to flambé a 1956 Fender Stratocaster.

When a friend of mine recovered the shards of a guitar from a Replacements show at Grinnell College in Iowa, I went to inspect the damage. He told me guitarist Bob Stinson had been wearing a tutu with a Betty Boop halter top and he'd already urinated off the stage before the destructive finale. I was impressed.

More than any intact vintage Fender or classic Gibson, a smashed guitar represents the most-prized collector's item from the ultimate rock'n'roll act of sacrifice. Yet upon further inspection, I was shocked to find out that the guitar destroyed by The Replacements was just a trashy old Hamer. Wasn't this sacrilegious? In ancient blood rituals wasn't the most beautiful virgin or the bravest warrior sacrificed—not some second-class citizen? Guitarist Bob Stinson—who was known for embellishing his band's feats—attempted a mitigating confession, claiming that the shattered Hamer was actually on loan to him.

In search of further guidance, the drummer from The Stardüsters and I sought the light at a Nirvana concert. At the end of the show, Nirvana half-heartedly trashed their instruments as though it was a tedious job required of all rock stars. Obviously the audience expected them to do it as though Nirvana was living out its lyrics from "Smells Like Teen Spirit": "Here we are now, entertain us!" And watching it all from the mosh pit in front of the band, I realized that

Kurt Cobain had set aside his beloved 1965 Fender Jaguar to smash a knock-off guitar. Wasn't that cheating? Musicians are supposed to put their heart and soul into their music; shouldn't the destruction of their instruments be heartfelt and spontaneous as well? When guitarists studiously plan to smash their axes, isn't that a farce?

Nirvana was redeemed in my eyes, however, when they mocked the audience in Seattle at the end of a concert. Cobain and company acted as if they were going to smash their guitars, but over the feedback from their pickups, they carefully disassembled their instruments with power tools.

I soon realized that only rich rockers could afford to destroy their instruments. This became painfully obvious when my band, The Stardüsters, landed one of our first gigs, playing at the Macalester College cafeteria. With their noses in their textbooks, studying students munched on hamburgers and tried to ignore the racket we were making. During the intermission, a student asked if he could play a song he was sure would go over with the indifferent crowd. We gave up our "stage," and he performed the two-chord Mexican hit "Tequila" alone on his own out-of-tune guitar. Students held their ears and attempted to concentrate ever harder on their studies as the guitarist strummed the strings ever louder for attention. After he shouted

GUITAR SMASHING LESSON
Opposite page: Pete Townshend fine-tunes the tone of his amp with the business end of his Stratocaster.

"Tequila" for the second time, he unstrapped his guitar and pummeled it into a pulp. The students finally looked up from their books, horrified. Silence reigned as all eyes fell on the musician, who stood embarrassed over the strings and splinters that had been his guitar. One of the disgusted students asked, "What on earth are you doing?" Not knowing what to do for an encore, the guitarist-without-a-guitar ran out the door in humiliation.

Smashing guitars suddenly seemed like a tired cliché, especially to jaded college students. We needed something fresh for Vinnie & The Stardüsters. When shooting the cover for our CD, the photographer suggested we strip and jump around, using our guitars to hide our unmentionables. Rather than banging our guitars on stage as on the cover of The Clash's *London Calling*, we jumped around naked with our guitars as figurative fig leaves. Even this plan backfired, however, when audiences at every show expected us to disrobe. We glumly took clothes off as the crowd hooted and hollered. Just like Pete Townshend's smashing of countless Rickenbackers, stripping needed to be spontaneous.

To avoid Vinnie & The Stardüsters becoming a skin-and-bones imitation of uninspired Chippendales, we needed new guitar tricks. I studied clips of Eddie Van Halen as he "shredded" the fretboard with hammer-ons and pull-offs to play a Bach fugue—finally my classical piano training proved useful. I repeatedly rewound a Stevie Ray Vaughan video to cop his technique for playing behind his back. When Vinnie & The Stardüsters finally got a show after the cafeteria debacle, I had my new guitar tricks in the bag. We played in a tiny basement jammed with beer drinkers and choked with cigarette smoke. In the middle of a rock anthem, I threw my guitar behind my back à la Stevie Ray, but instead it clunked to the floor when the strap popped off and feedback belched from the amp. I clumsily reattached my strap and acted like it was all intentional. The strap then broke and the borrowed guitar crashed on the ground once again. But to my surprise, the crowd cheered for this "spontaneous" rock'n'roll moment.

Spurred on by slam dancers spinning to our rock version of "The Barber of Seville"—with some Eddie Van Halen–like hammer-ons—I leaped into the air on the final note just like I'd seen Tommy Stinson from The Replacements do so many times. Unfortunately, the ceiling of this cellar was lower than I had counted on. My head crashed into an air duct and I fell back into a borrowed Marshall stack amp spilling five glasses of keg beer into the speakers. When I looked up, there was the owner of the amplifier glaring down at me. Not knowing what to do next, us Stardüsters hightailed it

1968 FENDER TELECASTER PAISLEY
The 1960s were in full glory when Fender glued wallpaper to its Telecaster body, covered it in acrylic, and released the paisley Telecaster. Suddenly, the Tele, that supreme working-class guitar, had gone flower power. Owner: Buck Sulcer. (Photograph © *Vintage Guitar*)

upstairs before he could grab us—and the basement crowd loved it! Just then, the police came through the front door responding to a neighbor's noise complaint. While the owners of the house promised the officers that they henceforth would be quieter, we ran out the back.

For days afterwards, I dared not answer the phone for fear of being hounded by the house tenants demanding to be reimbursed for damages. The guitar I borrowed for the show was stolen, so I had to buy a replacement for the owner. All the money I had saved for a new guitar went to buy one that I never even had a chance to desecrate!

Yet this disastrous show turned out to be a hit. That basement beer bash was our 1967 Monterey Pop Festival as word got around about how crazy and destructive Stardüster shows were. We were immediately "booked" to play other keg parties. Stardom was looming for The Stardüsters.

But at our next show, the audience demanded we smash our instruments and pour beer into our amps. Not able to afford new guitars and amps for each and every kegger, we just played our songs "straight." The crowd yelled at us, chided us, and then finally left in disappointment.

But we'll be back. I'm working on playing my guitar behind my head and with my teeth. And perhaps someday Vinnie & The Stardüsters will go on tour and can graduate to the ultimate rock'n'roll cliché—trashing hotel rooms.

GUITAR ANTICS

"Charley Patton was a clowning man with a guitar. He'd be in there putting his guitar all between his legs, carry it behind his head, lay down on the floor, and never stopped picking."
—Bluesman Sam Chatmon

"Things were always jumping, and the chicks would be excited. You'd see them crossing the floor, climbing the bandstand, and handing T-Bone money. Five and even tens! When he went into the splits, they'd kneel beside him, counting out their bills, putting them in his pockets or guitar! They'd call out requests and snap their fingers as they sturtted on back to their seats. People went wild. We never let him quit till the wee, wee hours."
—A fan remembering T-Bone Walker's 1940s guitar antics quoted in Helen Oakley Dance's *Stormy Monday: The T-Bone Walker Story*

"Earl Hooker, Matt Murphy, Magic Slim, Freddy King, Luther Allison—these guys were playing so much guitar, something told me, 'Don't even take your guitar out of the case.' But then something would tell me, 'Take it out of the case, hook it behind your back or put it behind your head. Just do anything to make somebody pay attention to you.' I was doing something different. . . . I had a long, 150-foot cord and I was sticking my guitar up in the roof and walking away and leaving it and laying it on the ground with the G-string open. And they was saying, 'What the hell is he doing?' I'd say, 'I'm doing something you guys ain't.'"
—Buddy Guy quoted in Donald E. Wilcox and Buddy Guy's *Damn Right I've Got The Blues*

"It used to frustrate me incredibly. I used to try and make up visually for what I couldn't play as a musician. . . . Instead I said, 'All right, you're not capable of doing it musically, you've got to do it visually.' I became a huge, visual thing. In fact, I forgot all about the guitar because my visual thing was more my music than the actual guitar. I got to jump about, and the guitar became unimportant. I banged it and I let it feed back and scraped it and rubbed it up against the microphone, did

T-BONE SHUFFLE
T-Bone Walker does the splits with his blonde Gibson ES-5 behind his head—a lesson that Jimi Hendrix learned well.

anything; it wasn't part of my act, even. It didn't deserve any credit or any respect. I used to bang it and hit it against walls and throw it on the floor at the end of the act."
—Pete Townshend, *The Rolling Stone Interviews: 1967–1980*

"We weren't content to just stand there and strum our guitars. That wasn't enough. We wanted to make a big splash."
—Gene Simmons, *KISS and Make-Up*

"At the end of the show, I threw my Danelectro up into the air and let it bounce up and down a few times until it broke. I thought that was the ultimate in glamor."
—Dee Dee Ramone, *Lobotomy: Surviving the Ramones*

"I guess I've never considered musical equipment very sacred. I've probably broken three hundred guitars."
—Kurt Cobain, *Guitar Player* magazine

"I'm a rotten guitar player if I'm standing still."
—Angus Young

The Gnarly Guitar Hall of Fame

By Dan Forte

Dan Forte, an ASCAP/Deems Taylor Award recipient for excellence in music journalism, joined the staff of Guitar Player *magazine in 1976. Over the next twelve years, he held the positions of assistant editor, senior associate editor, and editor at large at the magazine. He also served as editor at large for* Guitar World, *and wore the hats of compiler and annotator for the Legends of Guitar series of CDs on Rhino Records. Over the years, Dan has interviewed such guitar luminaries as Eric Clapton, Stevie Ray Vaughan, Frank Zappa, James Jamerson, and George Harrison. He is currently editorial consultant for* Vintage Guitar *magazine, where his "Check This Action" column appears monthly.*

There have been countless articles written about the heroes and virtuosos of the guitar, the fastest, most complex and most popular. But the guitarists I've always been attracted to are the slightly left-field players—the ones whose playing is so unexpected, over-the-top, and twisted, it stops you dead in your tracks. I'm not talking about the avant-garde school; these individualistic stylists crop up in all genres, in all eras. Some of them *are* virtuosos, some are even gods, but they've exhibited that wigged-out, gnarly streak from time to time—or in some cases <u>all</u> the time.

To start at the beginning, or darn close to it, there's "Rock Around the Clock" by Bill Haley & the Comets. Sure, you've heard it two billion times, but ever try playing that guitar break? That's Danny Cedrone, the accomplished, swing-influenced guitarist who

1965 FENDER STRATOCASTER
Every guitar has its signature tone, but few boast such a wide variety of voices as the Stratocaster. This stock sunburst Strat leans against a 1965 Fender 1x12 extension cabinet and 1964 blackface Fender Vibroverb. Owner: Cartwright Thompson. (Photograph © *Vintage Guitar*)

preceded the Comets' great Fran Beecher. And even hotter than that 1955 smash (actually cut in '54) was Haley & the Saddlemen's "Rock The Joint" from 1952, with Cedrone playing the exact same solo, note for note, with even more heat.

Johnny "Guitar" Watson started out as a pianist, but I think we'd all agree that Johnny "Piano" Watson just doesn't have the same cachet. After switching instruments, not quite nineteen years old, he cut "Space Guitar" in 1954, and blasted off. Basically a jump blues instrumental with stop-time breaks, Watson's use of studio reverb (really the only "effect" available in those days) and sheer off-the-wall madness (sliding wildly up the neck, repeatedly beating a bend into submission, throwing in the theme from *Dragnet*) transforms the piece into something truly out of this world, then or now. His scatter-shot bursts on "Three Hours Past Midnight" were enough to make Frank Zappa "just want to take an icepick and work over the neighborhood." A good collection of his work can be found on Rhino's *The Very Best Of Johnny "Guitar" Watson*, but it contains a re-recorded, 1963 version of "Those Lonely, Lonely Nights"; the original, and still best, version was his 1955 hit single for RPM, wherein he hammers the opening note of his solo 25 times in a row to make his point.

Country wizard Jimmy Bryant was supposedly difficult to work with in the studio, but one listen to *Two Guitars Country Style*, his 1954 masterpiece with steel guitarist Speedy West, is ample proof that he had a sense of humor. Jimmy and Speedy were perfectly matched for each other, and were such incredible players that they could joke around (or sound like they were) and still play stuff that had you shaking your head in wonderment. Bryant's guitar of choice in early years was a Telecaster, although he employed a Stratosphere Twin double-neck on "Stratosphere Boogie," which ended up on 1960's *Country Cabin Jazz*. With its twelve-string neck tuned in major and minor thirds, instead of octave, it gave the effect of an echo, with a harmonized line chasing the melody.

Of all the cool licks and hooks that Chuck Berry ever played, his first single, 1955's "Maybellene," remains the rawest. His jacked-up guitar break barely even resembles a guitar; it sounds more like a rocket

with the headers uncorked. No wonder parents were afraid of this new-fangled rock'n'roll music.

We have Elvis Presley to thank for the off-the-rails guitar break on his 1957 hit "Too Much." Sure, Scotty Moore played it, but The King insisted on leaving the warts-and-all track alone over Scotty's objections. Scotty's main influences were country greats Chet Atkins and Merle Travis, with a dose of B. B. King's blues thrown in—making him the perfect guitarist for Elvis' mix of country and rhythm and blues (a.k.a. rock'n'roll). On "Too Much" he clearly starts off with a worked-out little chromatic riff, but when he begins to deviate from it, he just plain loses his place—but, luckily, keeps going, to the point where he's just goofing, no doubt figuring, "No one is ever going to hear this." Guess again, Scotty.

With his 1958 hit "Rumble," Link Wray represented the lunatic fringe churches had been warning parents about. And onward to his almost metal take on "It's All Over Now, Baby Blue" in '79 and the ear-splitting live shows the septuagenarian puts on today, Link still embodies all that is gritty and mean and dangerous in rock'n'roll. He didn't strum the guitar; he thrashed, pummeled and beat it senseless. Other gems of simplicity and craziness are 1960's hyperventilating "Ain't That Lovin' You, Baby," 1961's squealing "Run Chicken Run," and 1962's whammy-yanking "Big City After Dark." His hypnotic "Jack the Ripper" from '63 was featured in the movies *Breathless* and *Desperado* and used in a Taco Bell commercial. *Yo quiero Link!*

Guitarists familiar with Ike Turner's early Kings of Rhythm work would no doubt cite "Prancin'" (from 1959, available on Ace's *Ike's Instrumentals*) as perhaps the ultimate example of his technique of employing the Stratocaster's whammy bar. But when Ike went back to his roots and toured behind his 2001 release, *Here and Now*, players were in for a shock. Those wild, exaggerated shimmies were almost all done with just finger vibrato; he only occasionally touched the wang bar. (If I didn't see it myself, I never would have believed it.)

Mickey Baker was a super-prolific '50s R&B session guitarist, author of a popular jazz guitar method book, and one half of the hit-making Mickey & Sylvia. His 1959 solo album for Atlantic, *The Wildest Guitar*, lived up to its title, on unexpected arrangements of jazz

I LIKE IKE
Stratocaster-toting Ike Turner and band.

standards like "Old Devil Moon." But he got even wilder on pianist Sammy Price's album *Rib Joint*.

"Train Kept A-Rollin'" by Johnny Burnette and The Rock 'N' Roll Trio is often cited as an early example of distorted rock guitar—with Paul Burlison's now-famous story of dropping his amp and accidentally loosening one of its power tubes. That may be true, but Burlison also occasionally joined Howlin' Wolf's band, whose radio slot was right next to his show on KWEM in West Memphis, Arkansas. And Wolf's original guitarist, Willie Johnson, was overdriving amps well before Burnette & Co. cut "Train" in '56. What's more radical than the distortion (however it was achieved) is the fact that Burlison plays the whole song by plucking octaves on the low and high E strings while fingering those two strings, and only those strings, with his left-hand thumb and index, up and down the neck.

Joining and then replacing Johnson in Wolf's band was Hubert Sumlin, whose unique approach to blues guitar was the perfect accompaniment to Wolf's powerful growl for more than two decades. On 1961's "Going Down Slow" his stinging tone leaps off the grooves, above Henry Gray's piano and Willie Dixon's spoken introduction. His out-of-phase fills and solo elevate 1963's "Three Hundred Pounds of Joy" from what could have been a mere novelty tune. And he delivers perhaps his most extroverted, notey lead on "Hidden Charms" from that same year. Hubert and Willie Johnson are *both* playing on "Smokestack Lightning," and similarly Sumlin shared guitar duties on "Killing Floor" with Buddy Guy and on "Shake For Me" with Jimmy Rogers. Yes, people, once upon a time not only did gods walk the earth, they got together and jammed at Chess Studios in Chicago.

Without a doubt, Buddy Guy's most flipped-out playing is on his 1968 live album *This Is Buddy Guy*—and, brother, that's saying something! Four cuts from that LP are included on Vanguard's Buddy compilation *As Good As It Gets*, along with an untitled slow blues instrumental from the same gig that outshines the lot, but was somehow previously unreleased. At his best, Buddy is all unbridled energy and emotion, taking ridiculous chances and hitting bull's eyes. At his worst, he can place showmanship (of the jive variety) above musicianship, and it can get mighty sloppy. Another of his on-target curve-ball leads is behind Junior Wells on "Vietcong Blues" (from the *Chicago/The Blues/Today* series), although the call-and-response he gets into with Junior singing about his "Stomach Ache" is hard to beat. (Both Wells tracks are on Junior's *Best Of The Vanguard Years*.)

Booker T. & The MG's' Steve Cropper is *the* master rhythm guitarist of R&B (check out "Hang 'Em High" as but one example), and when he stepped up to solo, what he lacked in flash he made up for in bite. The group's first hit, 1962's "Green Onions," was a major inspiration for Jeff Beck and supplied one of the most inspired meldings of celluloid and rock'n'roll, as the soundtrack for the grudge-match drag race between John Milner's yellow Deuce Coupe and Bob Falfa's black '55 Chevy, as the sun came up on Paradise Road in *American Graffiti*. Cropper's stiletto bends are enough to make you twinge, but he gets even more aggressive and lowdown on "Red Beans and Rice" (the flipside of the 1965 non-hit "Be My Lady").

As Ray Davies puts it, his younger brother Dave played guitar, especially when the Kinks were starting out, the way he talked—or rather, cussed. I can attest to that, having interviewed him for *Guitar Player* magazine in 1977. "Jimmy Page did not play the guitar solo on 'You Really Got Me,'" Dave volunteered. "That's really a lie. I guess it must be really important for him to say that." Now insert as many swear words as you can in that short quote, and you'll have an idea

of what he *really* said—blurted out with the same pent-up, seventeen-year-old aggression with which he thrashed his manic solo on the 1964 classic. On the session, Dave played a Harmony Meteor through a green El Pico amp. "I took one of my father's speakers," he recounted, "and slashed the back of the speakers." The El Pico was then used as a preamp with a Vox AC-30. There are still, no doubt, those who subscribe to Page's claim, despite Dave's pithy protestations, as well as testimonials from Ray Davies and producer Shel Talmy, the exhaustive *You Really Got Me: An Illustrated World Discography of The Kinks, 1964–1993* by Doug Hinman, and live footage of Dave playing that solo, spot on—even though the guitar work doesn't display any of Page's trademarks. (Which is not to say that Page isn't a great guitarist with a gnarly streak. Check out his nasal bends on "Hurdy Gurdy Man" and "Sunshine Superman" by Donovan.)

Of Eric Clapton's Yardbirds tenure, rock critic Dave Marsh once wrote, "There is little in his early recordings to substantiate claims of genius"—pointing out that he played Chuck Berry riffs with only as much skill as Keith Richards. But if anybody was getting the kind of tone and sustain E.C. achieved on "Good Morning Little Schoolgirl" (cut in '64; originally on *For Your Love*), no recordings have ever surfaced. Slowhand starts his solo bending up to the B, which he squeezes thirty-two times in a row, before releasing in a flourish that displays the melodic sense that would remain a Clapton hallmark—all in twenty seconds flat.

Still, when he vacated the band in early 1965, Jeff Beck stepped in with a take-no-prisoners, in-your-face attitude and an ear for the experimental, and raised the bar of lead guitar for all who followed. If you erected a Gnarly Guitar Hall of Fame, one wing would have to be devoted to Beck—in particular, his Yardbirds and *Truth* album periods. Clapton had dished up some Bo Diddley-inspired chicken-scratch sound effects on rave-ups like "Here 'Tis," but on the Yardbirds' revved-up take on Bo's "I'm a Man," Beck explored previously

1999 FENDER BROADCASTER AND GRETSCH BROADKASTER
When Leo Fender re-launched his two-pickup electric solid body with new neck truss rod as the Broadcaster in 1950, he was soon curtailed in using the name by Gretsch, who had already launched its Broadkaster drum set. Times change, and in 2002, Fender bought out Gretsch. The Broadcaster and Broadkaster were now part of the same company. (Photograph © *Vintage Guitar*)

HAIL ROCK'N'ROLL
Chuck Berry puts his good old Gibson
ES-350 to new uses.

uncharted sonic territory. Suddenly teenage kids cared more about being the guy *behind* the lead singer—the cool-as-ice hired gun with an electric guitar. If Hendrix created a never-imagined soundscape with few effects, Beck arguably did more with less—and did much of it more than a year prior. Pretty much everything Beck did with the band was daring and brilliant—"I'm Not Talking," "Train Kept A-Rollin'," "Shapes of Things," "You're a Better Man Than I," and, of course, the showboating "Jeff's Boogie."

For "Heart Full of Soul," bassist Paul Samwell-Smith recalled in 1986, "We tried a sitar player; we got a little Indian guy who was playing in London somewhere. He tried to play 'Heart Full of Soul' with us in ordinary, Western, straight 4/4 time—and he just couldn't do it." After trying his hand at the sitar, "Beck, who was a natural mimic and a great guitar player, just picked up his guitar and played as if he were playing the sitar," Paul explains. The Indian influence remained, with more sitar-inspired licks on "Over Under Sideways Down" and an ear-splitting solo on

"Hot House of Omagarashid." In late '66, Beck and Jimmy Page shared the lead chair for the psychedelic "Happenings Ten Years Time Ago," and on his own Beck put his Les Paul through the ringer on *Truth*'s "I Ain't Superstitious." (On the reformed Yardbirds' 2003 release, *Birdland*, ex-Dr. Feelgood guitarist Gypie Mayo continues the band's tradition of stellar lead men, as on "Please Don't Tell Me 'Bout the News.")

The wildest band of the Northwest scene that produced the Kingsmen and Paul Revere & the Raiders was the Sonics. On "The Witch" lead guitarist Larry Parypa sounds like Lonnie Mack on Benzedrine, with that same Magnatone vibrato, cranked up to spin cycle. Although it was eons in coming, the Sonics eventually got their due, with a boxed set of their entire Etiquette catalog and even a tribute album, featuring artists who were in diapers when the Sonics were around, doing Sonics classics like "Psycho" and "Strychnine."

Speaking of Lonnie Mack, seldom in the history of rock'n'roll (or the electric guitar) has an artist of such originality sprung totally formed, seemingly out of nowhere. The native Indianan had undoubtedly logged a gazillion miles and as many hours on the club-and-frat circuit before he got his big break at the end of someone else's recording session. He cut an instrumental treatment of Chuck Berry's "Memphis"—which ironically made Mack (who also happens to be one of the most soulful *singers* in the history of rock) an instrumental star. His aptly titled "Chicken Pickin'" was the blueprint for Stevie Ray Vaughan's "Scuttle Buttin'" and "Travis Walk." (To hear the source of another of Stevie's workouts, "Rude Mood," check out Lightnin' Hopkins' "Hopkins' Sky Hop," sometimes known as "Move On Out." To hear what Lonnie Mack would sound like at fast speed on a 45 with the hole off-center, get Travis Wammack's "Scratchy.")

Blue Cheer has historically been short-shrifted (even maligned) for being one-dimensional, unsophisticated, and most of all loud. To which I say, what's your point? In the bigger-is-better days of rock, circa 1968, the trio carted six Marshall double-stacks on stage—three each for guitarist Leigh Stephens and bassist Dickie Peterson—and from the sound of their debut, *Vincebus Eruptum*, they probably used the same

CHARLES K. RAMSDEN

Virtuoso of the Guitar, Presenting His
Musical Novelties

Featuring His Own Invention
The Electronic Novatar, Sensational, Revolutionary
Solo Instrument—Only One of Its Kind in the World
Product of 25 Years' Experimentation

Reproducing
An Amazing Variety of Musical and Sound Effects
Violin…Bag Pipes…Trumpet…Pipe Organ…Vibra Harp…
Drums…Animals…Trains and Many Others

Time _____

Place _____

Southern School Assemblies—Harry Byrd Kline, Director—Dallas, Texas

MUSICAL NOVELTIES
Forgotten guitar hero Charles K. Ramsden and his sensational, revolutionary Novatar.

setup in the studio. Like many at the time, Stephens' guitar of choice was a Gibson SG Standard. As much or more than anything that preceded it, the band's blistering, feedback-punctuated version of Eddie Cochran's "Summertime Blues," presaged heavy metal.

Jimi Hendrix's four-minute "Woodstock Improvisation"—his largely unaccompanied, brilliant "Malaguena"-like noodling—comes after the end of "Purple Haze" on the double *Live At Woodstock* CD. When Hendrix was booked to play the festival, his manager insisted he get top billing and close the show. Well, after delays due to rain and swelling crowds (approximately half a million), Jimi finally came on when the "Three Days of Peace & Music" was as good as over, at around 9:00 Monday morning, performing to an enormous field of garbage and a few crispy critters who didn't heed the warnings about the brown acid. Listen to Hendrix's stream-of-altered-consciousness meanderings and imagine what it sounded like to *them*.

Barry Melton may not have been the "best" guitarist of the psychedelic era, but he was easily the "most" psychedelic. His solo on Country Joe & the Fish's "Section 43" is a jagged, splattery flurry of quasi-Eastern licks, and a far cry from his (and his bandmates' folk) beginnings. The version on the group's debut album, *Electric Music for the Mind and Body*, is nice, but the quintessential rendition is from one of their do-it-yourself Rag Baby EPs, which have been collected on one CD, *Collector's Items: Their First Three EP's*.

The title song of Funkadelic's 1971 album, "Maggot Brain" consists of a sole rhythm guitar's arpeggiated descending minor chords, over which an uncredited lead guitarist showers a torrent of anguished fuzz. The lead guitarist and co-writer of the ten-minute tour de force was Eddie Hazel, and as the story goes, bandleader George Clinton instructed him to "play like your mama just died." The acid-blues solo Hazel

1960s FENDER STRATOCASTER TRIO

A lineup of custom-color Strats in front of a Fender Bandmaster. From left, a 1963 in Metallic Olive Drab; a 1965 Olympic White; and a 1965 Dakota Red. Owner: Ron De Marino. (Photograph © *Vintage Guitar*)

delivers is nasty and eloquent at the same time, holding its own alongside Hendrix at his best.

It amazes me when I run into people (sometimes journalists or would-be musicologists) who think that blues, by definition, is "sad music." To which I submit as Exhibit A, Hound Dog Taylor & The Houserockers—the ultimate party band, guaranteed to make you smile. Hound Dog preferred cheapo Japanese electrics with lots of chrome and switches, and he had one of the rawest, raspiest tones of any bottleneck-style slide player. He and drummer Ted Harvey and rhythm guitarist Brewer Phillips made such a racket, they didn't need a bass player. Check out 1971's "See Me In The Evening," from *Natural Boogie* (Alligator).

Harvey Mandel grew up the proverbial suburban kid being the only white person jamming in the steamy blues clubs of Chicago's South and West Sides. He emerged a total original, even on his earliest recordings, like Vanguard's *Stand Back! Here Comes Charley Musselwhite's South Side Band*, recorded in 1966, when Harvey was twenty-one. His fuzzed tone, unmatched sustain, and country-tinged bending techniques transcended the twelve-bar blues surroundings. Mandel's original instrumental "4 P.M." begins with short, choppy bursts before he lets his long, snakey lines unwind, and on "Chicken Shack" (in the days of vinyl) he repeats a riff just enough times to make you think your record is skipping.

When Maria Muldaur struck gold with "Midnight at the Oasis" in 1974, everyone (including greats such as Chet Atkins) stood up and took notice of the out-of-left-field, elegant solo by Amos Garrett. His seamless, multi-string bending technique is the closest anyone can come to Hawaiian steel guitar without using a slide. (I've seen the man perform live, and even though I *knew* he was getting those sounds with just his bare hands, I still had to do a double-take.) A good example of this is his adaptation of the Santo & Johnny oldie "Sleep Walk," from *I Make My Home In My Shoes*.

Multi-string instrumentalist David Lindley was *the* in-demand accompanist for the L.A. elite in the '70s,

before he launched his solo career (auspiciously with the pedal-to-metal steel guitar of *El Rayo-X*'s "Mercury Blues"). His tasteful lap steel became as integral a part of Jackson Browne's sound as the singer-songwriter's own voice. But on occasion, like on "That Girl Could Sing" (from Browne's *Hold Out*), Lindley could get crazy. With the tone of a seal at feeding time (thanks to a Fairchild limiter on its last legs), he played exactly what one *wouldn't* expect in the catchy tune. Lindley recalls hooking up a batch of effects to his Supro steel and playing: "'How's that sound?' 'Sounds like a seal.' 'Shit yeah, that's it. Roll the tape.'" As Jackson Browne says, "I love that solo, because it's like an anti-solo."

I was certain Neil Young would win the distortion sweepstakes with "Hey Hey, My My" or "My My, Hey Hey"—from either 1979's *Rust Never Sleeps* or 1991's *Weld*—but Nirvana somehow added an extra layer of fuzz on "Smells Like Teen Spirit," from 1991's *Nevermind*. Guess that's why they called it grunge. Based on one of the simplest, catchiest riffs in recent memory, the song explodes with Kurt Cobain's extreme bends and shouts of "Hey!" over and over.

The player who tops this list was a question mark until recently. You see, when Varese Sarabande released the soundtrack to Orson Wells' *Touch Of Evil* on CD in 1993, one could only speculate who the uncredited wildman with treble to spare could possibly be, playing his heart out on rockin' R&B intrumentals like "Orson Around" and "Lease Breaker," as part of Henry Mancini's score. The impassioned bends and crazed, angular lines didn't sound like anything that could come out of a typical "studio" player. This sounded like a battle to the death between Ike Turner and Johnny "Guitar" Watson—with Guitar Slim and Mickey Baker waiting in the wings. But whoever it was clearly had a street-level understanding of R&B with an obviously thorough grounding in harmony and theory.

Los Angeles's Musicians Union Local 47 FAX'ed me the actual contract from the date (January 17, 1958), and the guitar-slinger turned out to be one of

DOUBLE TROUBLE
Stevie Ray Vaughan and company.

STEVIE RAY VAUGHAN
AND
DOUBLE TROUBLE

★ ★ WITH SPECIAL GUEST ★ ★ ★
THE THUNDERBIRDS
SYRIA MOSQUE
PITTSBURGH, PENNSYLVANIA
FRI., JAN. 24th - 1986 ★ 7:30pm

(249)

TIPTOEING THROUGH THE TULIPS
Mild-mannered Herbert B. Correy won fame and fortune in the 1960s as Tiny Tim, with a string of hit novelty tunes powered by his trusty ukulele.

the greatest jazz guitarists of all time, Barney Kessel. I asked Barney what reservoir he was dipping into—because he obviously displayed an intimate understanding of what that music was about, but rarely showed this side of his personality. His response was, "It's out of me. It's my sound." Which may sound a little left-field considering this is the same guitarist playing the sophisticated chordal accompaniment to Julie London on "Cry Me a River," but it's worth noting that Barney began playing electric guitar at fourteen in 1937, in Ellis Ezell's all-black fourteen-piece orchestra in his hometown of Muskogee, Oklahoma—not too long after people like Eddie Durham and Charlie Christian introduced the instrument to jazz (and years before the likes of B. B. King). No doubt they were rockin'!

Inevitably, there's got to be some honorable mentions hurriedly crammed onto a grouping such as this, so read the following in the spirit (and at the speed) of Love Sculpture's "Sabre Dance" featuring Dave Edmunds. Also noteworthy are: "Reveille Rock" by Johnny & the Hurricanes, featuring Dave Yorko; Nashville session great Grady Martin's mega-fuzz as far back as Marty Robbins' 1961 hit, "Don't Worry"; Willie Joe & his Unitar one-stringing his way through "Unitar Rock," Rene Hall's "Twitchy" and Bob Landers' "Cherokee Dance"; too many to mention by Bo Diddley (but check out "Bo's Bounce"); Wild Jimmy Spruil showing how he got his nickname on Wilbert Harrison's "Kansas City"; Buckaroo Don Rich giving his Tele palpitations on Buck Owens' "My Heart Skips A Beat"; anything by Eddie "Guitar Slim" Jones, especially "Story Of My Life"; the Ventures' live-in-Japan version of "Caravan" (from *The Ventures On Stage*), featuring Nokie Edwards; Zoot Horn Rollo (Bill Harkleroad) and Antennae Jimmy Semens on Captain Beefheart's *Trout Mask Replica*; John Fahey's "Guitar Excursions into the Unknown"; Junior Brown utilizing both necks (and the low E's tuning peg) of his Guit-Steel on "Broke Down South of Dallas"; Frank Zappa's "Shut Up and Play Yer Guitar Some More"; Roy Buchanan's haunting volume swells on "Sweet Dreams" and his paint-peeling tone on the Bobby Gregg single "The Jam"; Richard Thompson at his most aggressive on "Can't Win" from the Hannibal/Rykodisc box, *Watching The Dark*; Junior Barnard's aggressive bluesiness with western swing king Bob Wills and brother Johnnie Lee Wills' band; the ahead-of-its-time jazz of Joe Cinderella on "Ironworks" from saxophonist Gil Melle's *Primitive Modern*; anything funky by Tony Joe White (especially if he's using a fuzztone or wah-wah); Ron Wood's "sounds like cat food smells" tone (to quote roots rocker Webb Wilder) on the Faces' "Borstal Boys"; John Cipollina on Quicksilver Messenger Service's "Cobra"; western jazzer Jimmie Rivers (with steel man Vance Terry) on *Brisbane Bop*; gospel star Sister Rosetta Tharpe's SG in overdrive (as in the video clip in the movie *Amelie*); human jukebox Snooks Eaglin's electric flamenco with a backbeat on "Funky Malaguena"; and, finally, Hilton Valentine strangling the same note twenty-two times on the Animals' "See See Rider."

So next time you're shopping for guitar music, think crazed, think wild, and, above all, think gnarly.

LOUDNESS IS NEXT TO GODLINESS

"What did Dick Dale do to change the course of rock? It wasn't just inventing a style of music, called 'surf music,' that every kid started following in that era. What he did was change the way music was played. Everybody in the '50s was limited and just harnessed to the electronics of the era. If you took somebody like Les Paul, who was playing at that time, and The Champs ['Tequila'], they were playing with stand-up acoustic basses. The electric guitar was not a loud item.

"In fact, the Telecaster had just been finished and perfected by Leo Fender, who was the Einstein and the god of guitars. Leo made the Telecaster for the chicken-plucking sound created by the country players. Everybody'd go 'Tickety-teoow!' And that kind of stuff. Nobody had an amplifier that went above 5, even though the dial went from 0 to 10. Chuck Berry and all these people were playing through 6-, 8-, 10-inch speakers. Some amp makers used to try to fool some of these kids. They'd go, 'Oh, look at this! Watch this! My volume control, the minute you hit 3, look at how loud it is!' People didn't realize that after you went past 3, it just went up to sheer distortion. But Leo had a graduated pot where it went all the way up to 10, and after about 8, then you were into the distortion range.

"So I said, 'Now, Leo, I gotta have a fat, thick sound.' He had given me this Stratocaster that had only been out a year. It was still in its virginistic approach. He says, 'Here, beat this to death and tell me what you think.' So I would take it and beat on it. And I said, 'Leo, I gotta have a louder, thicker sound!' So, we'd go into what we called the little laboratory room, and I'd be bangin' on the amps and speakers we had there. He would bring out a wall of speakers. It was a rolling wall that was about, maybe six feet high up and about eight feet long. They had a dozen or two speakers on it. It would sound loud, right there; then I would go up onstage. Well, after the first thousand people, the bass response would suck up; it just wasn't think and fat enough. Then I started blowing up these amps. I blew up over 40 to 50 amplifiers and speakers. The speakers would catch on fire. Leo said, 'Why do you have to be so loud?'

"Finally, one day Leo and Freddie [Tavares, Fender R&D man] were standing in the middle of 4,000 people, and Leo said, 'Now I know what Dick Dale is trying to tell me!' Back to the drawing board! He went back and made the first 85-watt output transformer that was ever shoved into an amplifier and called it the 'Dick Dale Transformer.' Then we needed a speaker to put it through. I blew up everything

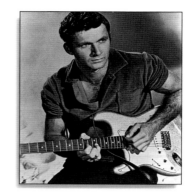

THE BEAST
Surf rocker Dick Dale and The Beast.

they had—the cones would just come straight out, they would twist, they would tear. Freddie would say, 'Dick! You can't do that, Dick! God, you can't keep doing that!' And, of course, I'm playing on .060 gauge strings.

"So, Leo and I go into the J.B. Lansing Co. [maker of JBL speakers] and we say, 'Look, we need a 15-inch speaker! We want a bigger birdcage! We want thicker windings, a bigger voice coil! And then I want an aluminum dust cover, so when you hit it with a pick, it gives you this ticking sound.' We also wanted them to put rubber glue around the front and the back edge of the speakers to help stop them from being torn out of the speaker casing. So, the Lansing people thought we were crazy. They said, 'What are you gonna put it on, a tugboat or something?' Leo said, 'Just do it, please.' It eventually became the 15-inch D-130F speaker.

"Leo released the first amp package commercially as the Showman amp. We took that speaker and put it in a 3-foot-high cabinet, 2 feet wide, and 12 inches deep. And then we hooked up the 85-watt output transformer. There was no sound portholes in the speaker cabinet. Now, that transformer peaked at 100 watts. That's when Dick Dale broke the sound barrier. Other players, they could only go to 5, no matter what they did. Well, Dick Dale went to 11!

"...When Dick Dale plugged that in, he not only broke the sound barrier, he went into a black hole and made those people's ears bleed! I was the first person in history to take six of those speakers, and six of those amplifiers, and in-line wire them all together. I hit the first note, and it raised me about four feet off the ground.

"Now, what did Dick Dale do to change the history of rock'n'roll? He became the Father of Loud."
—Dick Dale quoted in Greg Douglass' liner notes to *Better Shred Than Dead: The Dick Dale Anthology*

CHAPTER 4

Pop Songs
and Pop Culture

HARMONY
Junior and Sis prepare for their future career as music stars while Rover sings harmony.

Air Guitar Anatomy

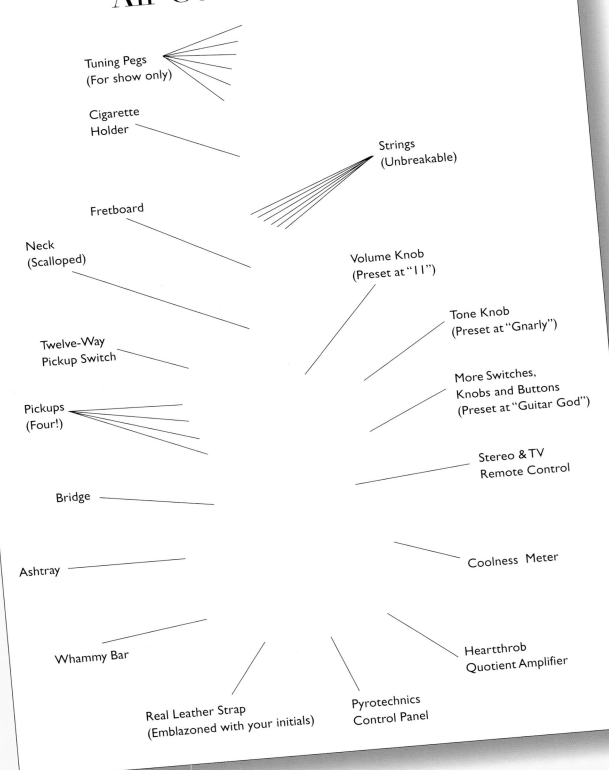

Tuning Pegs
(For show only)

Cigarette
Holder

Strings
(Unbreakable)

Fretboard

Neck
(Scalloped)

Volume Knob
(Preset at "11")

Tone Knob
(Preset at "Gnarly")

Twelve-Way
Pickup Switch

More Switches,
Knobs and Buttons
(Preset at "Guitar God")

Pickups
(Four!)

Stereo & TV
Remote Control

Bridge

Coolness Meter

Ashtray

Heartthrob
Quotient Amplifier

Whammy Bar

Real Leather Strap
(Emblazoned with your initials)

Pyrotechnics
Control Panel

Boy Diagnostics
What His Air Guitar Technique Tells You About Him

By Mikki Halpin

Mikki Halpin writes from experience. She's had her heart broken by several guitar players—but, thank god, no drummers. Mikki is the former editor-in-chief of the magazine Stim—*a now-defunct alternative effort labeled "the next* New Yorker" *in* Time *magazine. She currently serves as the deputy editor of* Seventeen *magazine and the editor-in-chief of* Weezer Singalong. *As Mikki notes, boys are mysterious creatures, but she has uncovered a smart new way to learn more about them.*

The Extremely Public Strummer

Technique: You're sitting in a bar, having a general get-to-know-you kind of conversation. Suddenly a lame Pearl Jam song comes on. Does your guy groan in disgust? Or at least remain silent? Or does he close his eyes, pick up the imaginary Stratocaster, and have at it like you aren't even there?

Analysis: The Extremely Public Strummer is more interested in making music with himself than with you. Key to his pleasure, though, is the public and performative aspect of his playing. In the romantic arena he tends to get crushes on unattainable girls whom he sees as queenbees, or important in his social circle. Thus he can yearn for them, and discuss his yearning for them with everyone ad nauseum, but never actually have a relationship.

Tip: Laugh in his face.

AIR GUITAR ANATOMY
Everything you'll ever need to know to operate your air guitar.

The Nietszchean Solo Artist

Technique: Around the house he plays a lot of music. Obscure noise like Yar Null and Zeni Geva, but also some cheesy guitar gods like Joe Satriani and Steve Vai. What the hell does he get up to, alone in his room with the music playing? Every time you walk in, he abruptly drops his hand to his lap and looks annoyed.

Analysis: The Nietzschean Solo Artist does not want to join a band or make any other commitments. He is highly creative and sensitive, but wholly focused on himself. He is often suspicious of others and fears that they might try to steal his essence, artistically speaking. Tends to have a lot of half finished projects—novels, grad school applications, etc.

Tip: The Nietzschean Solo Artist is often an oral sex superstar. Enjoy it while you can.

The Aimless Noodler

Technique: He's three hours late and you're getting annoyed. When you call, he makes small sheepish sounds and meekly explains that he was really getting into his new MIDI setup. You would have gone to the movies alone, had you known he was utilizing his computer skills to live out his adolescent fantasies.

Analysis: "Sheepish" is the key word here. This is the kind of guy who will forget to pay his bills for months, then whine about the mean companies trying to serve him for what he owes. The Aimless Noodler often feels that he is in a battle with time—it gets away from him, there is never enough of it, and he likes to feign productivity by staying up late.

Tip: He won't stray. As long as you can remain properly comforting (and gradually take over most of the responsibilities in his life), you've got the guy for good. Unless, of course, someone else who wants him more turns up the pressure: he cracks easily.

The Furtive Picker

Technique: Driving to a party, his favorite band comes on the car stereo. He keeps his hands on the wheel, in the correct ten and two o'clock position, except at red lights. Whenever the car is stopped, he leans back in

ROMANCE ON SIX STRINGS
Cisco Kid screen star Warner Baxter strums a romantic chord and wears his mustachio.

STAR EYES
Opposite page: The eyes tell all when diagnosing a boy.

his seat and lets a few riffs glide off his fingers. When the light changes, he resumes driving safely.

Analysis: The Furtive Picker doesn't really know how to have fun. He is always conscious of limits, boundaries. He secretly thinks that having multiple orgasms is a form of showing off. He's got his career planned to the most minute detail.

Tip: Your parents will love him.

The Boy in the Band

Technique: He's got a great bunch of guy friends and they hang out a lot. You're OK with that—you're secretly planning to set some of them up with your single friends. But they have an unnerving group-bonding ritual where they all play air guitar *together*.

Analysis: The Boy in the Band has some intimacy problems. Because no relationship can ever be as strong as the one with his buddies (or with the girls in his band, if any), he is unwilling to put any effort into one. When questioned about his feelings, he will react with confusion and hostility.

Tip: Join the band.

The Man Who Plays in Pain

Technique: He screws up his face in an orgiastic display while performing. Strangers often attempt to perform the Heimlich.

Analysis: The Man Who Plays in Pain secretly fears he will be exposed as a fraud. It doesn't matter if he isn't a fraud at all; he still fears exposure and will maintain an aura of deep passion at all times.

Tip: You want a tip for this guy? You want to see that face in bed?

The Flycatcher

Technique: Adds an open-mouthed twist to his playing, and always plays with that blank, deer-in-the-headlights look.

Analysis: The Flycatcher looks really stupid when he does this. Do we really need to analyze it for you?

Tip: Often trainable.

Romantic Riffs

Twelve Steps to Wooing the
One You Love with Your Guitar

By Margret Aldrich

Margret Aldrich lives in Minneapolis, Minnesota, with her uncle Kevin's 1966 Silvertone and a borrowed Supro amp. While she has wooed and been wooed by guitar players in the past, the person who won her heart is a non-musician who, as a stone-broke graduate student, sacrificed food and other amenities to get Margret her first acoustic guitar. To this day, he is kind enough to listen to her questionable renditions of classic Johnny Cash tunes.

Ask most people why they learned to play the guitar, and chances are they'll tell you it was to impress that special boy or girl who set their hearts aflutter. Generations of garage bands have formed over the years in thinly veiled attempts to charm a cheerleader, captivate the homecoming king, or attract the eye of the girl next door. And what better way to do it? Love potions don't exist, horoscopes can't offer celestial assistance to the dateless and the lonely, but anyone can learn to woo with the simple combination of six strings and three magic chords.

What is it about a guitar that can transform the most awkward teenager into a rock star and the most ordinary Joe into a guitar god? Science can't explain it, but the phenomenon has been around for years. Buddy Holly was encumbered by black, horn-rimmed glasses and unruly curls, but screaming girls flocked to his concerts and clamored for more. Prince stands only five feet, two inches tall, but holding a guitar on stage, he seems to rocket to a glittering, seven-foot giant cheered on by a legion of fans. Liz Phair is a plain Jane until she picks up an axe and strums her first, beautiful chord. You, too,

ROMANTIC RIFFS
Rudolph Valentino croons and his conquest swoons.

can learn how to woo masterfully with a guitar if you follow this elementary twelve-step program.

Step one: Remember that a guitar is the ultimate accessory. Using a guitar as a prop rivals all other fashion trends. Forget the Rolex or the leather Gucci shoulder bag. Don't bother with a manicure, five nights a week at the gym, or a designer haircut. Instead, strap on a Stratocaster.

My friend Carol, now a successful businesswoman of 29, was struck by the power of the guitar-as-killer-accessory at a young age. As we sipped Cosmos at a nightspot in Minneapolis's Warehouse District, she explained to me her first—but not last—experience dating guitar players. "My boyfriend from junior year of high school through sophomore year of college was a 'guitar god,'" she told me. "What this meant was he wore his hair long and had several guitars, amps, and other impressive-looking bits of equipment scattered throughout his bedroom and basement. Even though he mainly played electric, he was hardly ever in a band, being somewhat of a slacker in nature. I laugh looking back on it, but of course, at the time, just the fact that he occasionally cradled a guitar in his scrawny arms was enough to set my pulse racing."

It's true that you won't be able to have a guitar with you at all times, but you can remind the one you want to woo that, yes, you are a guitar player. Leave picks lying around your apartment. Use your amplifiers as furniture. Name your dog Les Paul or Marshall. Wear your calluses with pride.

Step two: Learn more than one song. If you're a beginner, it may be that you've mastered your first song but are so pleased by the accomplishment that you haven't moved on to song number two. While it's exciting to learn one piece well, show off your skills by adding a simple country love song or a jazz standard to your repertoire. Your beloved will be impressed by your range and thrilled not to have to sit through your nineteenth halting version of "Stairway to Heaven."

Step three: Use your guitar as a conversation piece. Being a guitarist doesn't mean you have to play like a pro. Sometimes the guitar itself and the idea of you playing it are enough to break the ice.

I learned this lesson when I picked up guitar as a teenager. My first 45 had been a copy of Joan Jett and the Blackhearts' "I Love Rock 'N Roll," and from that day forward, I was enamoured with the idea of becoming a tough-as-nails guitar player and wearing lots of black eyeliner. Unfortunately, I couldn't afford a guitar, and my parents didn't approve of too much makeup, but I did eventually talk the school band director into letting me claim a Fender and an old amp that no one was using. I would haul it home every weekend and soon realized that wooing the opposite sex with a guitar did not necessarily depend on how well you could play—or if you could play at all. The fact that I was seen carrying a guitar case through the halls of my high school was enough to ignite enthusiastic, sparkling conversation from the carefully nonchalant teenage boys who came up to me to say, "So. You play guitar. Cool."

Step four: Form a band as quickly as possible. For unexplained reasons, the allure of the guitar increases exponentially when it is played in a group setting. Your mere affiliation with band mates will make you more mysterious, interesting, and visible. Choosing an ambiguous or cryptic band name will help foster your new, fascinating persona.

Step five: Look for opportunities to perform with your band onstage. Performing live with a crowd of rowdy fans yelling their appreciation is key to boosting your guitar-god or -goddess status. The power of your guitar-playing will be intensified in direct ratio to the number of eyes watching you. If your band is just starting out, it's not a bad idea to add a few well-placed fans to the horde. If you have good-looking siblings, or a few loyal friends who are willing to do you a favor, put them in the front row and request high-decibel screaming. Make T-shirts screen-printed with your group's name and beg your buddies to wear them. Plaster band-name bumper stickers and posters on streetlamps around town. The person you're wooing will wonder what all the fuss is about.

Step six: Play with intensity. Even the most

TANTALIZING UKULELE
Step one in wooing: Remember that a guitar—or in some cases, uke—is the ultimate accessory.

1950s BUSATO DUO

In France, Italian immigrant luthier Mario Maccaferri sparked a revolution with his *modèle jazz* guitar designed for Paris' Henri Selmer & Cie. With an internal resonating box on the earliest models, steel strings, a cutaway body, and a trebly tone that could make itself heard in jazz bands, the Selmer became the guitar of choice for Manouche Gypsy legend Jean "Django" Reinhardt. Soon, other Paris-based Italian luthiers were offering their own versions, including the esteemed guitars made by Bernabe "Pablo" Busato, such as this early 1950s *petite* and *grande bouche* duo. Owner: Michael Dregni.

intelligent people find a guitarist who plays with deep-down, soul-searching, eyes-shut angst hard to resist. Shelly, a happening graduate student and librarian in her early thirties, passes along this tale of the allure of passionate guitarists . . .

"A few years ago, I dated a guy who was several years my junior (I was 29, he was 22). He liked to drink a lot, and he happened to be a guitar player. A very good guitar player, as a matter of fact. One night, I brought him to an after-hours party at a friend's house where someone brought out a guitar. After politely listening to other people's three-chord misadventures, he asked if he could play something. He started playing one of his original, Tom Waits–inspired songs—really tearing it up—and I noticed that people began to pay attention to him. The next thing I noticed was blood running down the front of my friend's acoustic guitar. My date was playing so hard that his fingers were bleeding. It was a little gross, and it certainly must have annoyed my friend to have a stranger's blood all over his guitar, but it also made him so palpably sexy and primal that I think some of my friends in the room who previously found him to be more trouble than he was worth kind of got the appeal."

Step seven: Don't be too intense. While bloody fingers and self-involved playing can be somehow attractive, overly excessive passion can have the opposite result. Don't overdo it with guitar theatrics, and don't succumb to a fit of facial contortions. Looking mad, fervent, disgusted, or bored when you play the guitar is fine, but looking as if you are in a fit of demonic possession or suffering the toxic effects of a strong poison is not. If you aren't sure how much facial contortion is too much, look in the mirror and ask yourself this simple question: Am I making a face that one would regularly see on Carlos Santana during a solo? If the answer is yes, you may want to tone it down.

Step eight: Avoid guitarist trappings. The fashion stylings of our guitar heroes can be a bad influence. Lace-up pants, shirts unbuttoned to the navel, and fringed sleeves are almost never flattering. Above all, beware of band hair. Anything taller than four inches, or anything that resembles a mullet, may greatly lessen your chances in winning the heart of your sweetheart-to-be. Remember, this isn't 1985, and you are not Eddie Van Halen or Nancy Wilson. In times of confusion, repeat this mantra: "Pick your guitar, not your hair."

Step nine: Write a song with his or her name in it. Perhaps one of the reasons a musician holds so much appeal is that there is a slight chance said musician could immortalize your very name in a song. The Rolling Stones' "Angie," the Velvet Underground's "Sweet Jane," Concrete Blonde's "Joey," and Elvis Costello's "Alison" are a few of the countless examples of this strategy. A personalized song can possess a lot of clout, so, if you can, polish your singing voice, turn down the volume on your amp, and put your darling's name in an original ballad, written by you.

With a name like "Margret," I haven't had much luck getting it into the title of a love song. When it has been attempted, the closest rhymes found were things like "target," and "TV set." To avoid troublesome monikers, feel free to substitute "girl," or "boy" for your subject's name—but be sure to tell the lucky one whom the song is about. This works almost as well.

Step ten: Make a tape of yourself for your beloved. While absence can make the heart grow fonder, absence plus a recording of you playing the guitar can make the heart grow much fonder, much faster. Jason, a friend of mine from college, took a field-research position in South America after graduation that was to last six months. While he was there, he learned to play guitar and sent a tape of his virtuosity to Jen, the woman he had been dating when he left home. She tells me that her roommate would laugh whenever she played it because there was such a long, drawn-out pause between each chord change, but Jen wore that tape out, and today she and Jason are married. Behold the power of the axe!

Step eleven: Show him or her how to play a few chords. You and your sweetheart touching hands as you instruct on the perfect fingering for the D chord. Need I say more?

Step twelve: Don't love your guitar more than you love

FRED HESS & SON
NO-1405

DOBRO CHIMES
The plaintive wail of the dobro courts a countrified sweetie.

HAWAIIAN SERENADE
Opposite page: The soothing sounds of the Hawaiian isles was music to woo by. This band was outfitted with a full range of rare Rickenbacker electrics, from Frying Pan lap steels to horseshoe-pickup four- and six-string Spanish electrics.

that special someone. There's nothing worse than a romance between a guitarist and his or her guitar that goes too far. Some tell their significant others they need "quality time" with their guitars and proceed to lock themselves in a room with their Gibson for hours—or days. Some fixate on keeping their living quarters at the perfect humidity; others spend inordinate amounts of time on the upkeep of their guitars; yet others scour guitar shops, flea markets, and pawn shops every weekend, searching for a vintage amp or a seasoned National to add to their harem of instruments.

Loving your guitar is not a crime. Just remember that the one you woo should always come first, if you want to get and keep the boy or girl. And isn't that why you learned to play in the first place?

CHAPTER 5

Mythology

1966 RICKENBACKER 370/12
A three-pickup new-style Rick 370/12 awaits. (Photograph
© *Vintage Guitar*)

Bizarre Guitars

The Electric Guitar as the Icon of the Twentieth Century

By Teisco Del Rey

Teisco Del Rey was the first writer to shine a light on those basement beauties of guitardom that had previously been left in the dark. His June 1983 feature for Guitar Player, "Cheap Thrills & Pawnshop Prizes," received an overwhelming reader response and resulted in Teisco's monthly column, "Off the Wall," which ran for the next eleven years. Teisco (who is related in spirit only to the Japanese guitar company that shares his name) can today be heard playing a variety of electric guitars and the Guitorgan on his two critically acclaimed instrumental CDs, The Many Moods of Teisco Del Rey *and* Teisco Del Rey Plays Music for Lovers.

Several years ago—in 1985, to be exact—I attended a fascinating exhibit at the Whitney Museum in New York City, called "High Styles." It featured dozens of examples of functional art with not necessarily functional designs, dating from early America to (at that time) the present. There were examples of Shaker furniture, art deco radios, pencil sharpeners from the '50s shaped like rocket ships, and even an Apple IIc computer.

But what struck me, and what has stuck with me all these years since, was what the exhibit left *out*. Because, to me, if you wanted to cite one object to symbolize the last half of the Twentieth Century, you'd be hard-pressed to come up with a more appropriate icon than the electric guitar. It reflected changing times as vividly as hem lines, hair styles, furniture, architecture, or this year's Cadillac. Art, fashion, progress, conflict, the Generation Gap—it was all embodied in that hunk of wood with steel strings and magnetic pickups. Or in some cases, hunk of plastic, Masonite, Res-o-glas, metal, aluminum, or just

BIZARRO
Guitarslinger Teisco Del Rey and friends show off the latest in bizarre guitar ware and wear. From left, a twelve-string Vox Mando-Guitar, Murph twelve-string, and Hallmark Swept-Wing. (Photograph courtesy Teisco Del Rey)

about anything else you could attach a neck and strings to. And, as with some of the examples on exhibit at the Whitney, design was not always a product of function or even common sense. Of course, electric guitars were around during the *first* half of the century as well, but it was after pioneers like Leo Fender, Paul Bigsby, "App" Appleton, Doc Kaufman, and others perfected their experiments with *solidbody* electric guitars that things kicked into high gear. Before long it was anything goes, in terms of design.

When I was a kid, an "electric guitar" was something to *ooh* and *ahh* over. It was something worth turning the TV on to hear and look at. Well after the arrival of rock'n'roll, into the early '60s, it was rare to see one in person, rarer still to know somebody who actually owned one. Anybody who owned an electric guitar, you figured, must also have a life-sized Robbie the Robot doing the dishes and a hovercraft parked in the garage.

Had I been a few years older, the saxophone might have stirred my imagination, via hits like "Tequila" by the Champs or "Honky Tonk" by Bill Doggett's combo. But when I was barely five, Duane Eddy came on the radio, and equally important on TV, with "Rebel-'Rouser." He didn't sing; he didn't have to. He just stood there and looked cool—and twanged the low strings on that *electric guitar*. Sure, I'd seen and heard rock'n'roll played on electric guitar before, but instead of being the guy standing *behind* Ricky Nelson or Elvis Presley, Duane and his guitar took center stage. And that tremolo coming out of the amplifier and those wobbly dips he made the notes do with that chrome bar—you couldn't do that on some little cowboy acoustic.

As I write this, I'm forty-nine years old, and virtually my entire professional life has been connected to the electric guitar—playing it, writing about it, collecting guitars, and interviewing the instrument's biggest stars and unsung heroes. (Along the way, I even met and became friends with Duane Eddy.) That's a pretty profound effect for an "object" to have on one's life, and I know I'm not alone.

Leo Fender's idea was to make an electric Hawaiian guitar that could be played like a "Spanish," fretted guitar, instead of with a slide. And he did it in about the simplest, most obvious way imaginable. Don't forget: This is the same mind who decided that the upright bass player should be freed up to do dance steps with the rest of the band, and so invented the Fender Precision bass. (The revolutionary impact it would have musically was the furthest thing from his mind.) The body of the Broadcaster/Esquire (later re-named the Telecaster) was far from sexy; it was pretty much a butcher block with a fairly wide "waist," so you could rest it on your knee while playing, and a cutaway, to give easier access to the higher frets. Bruce Springsteen called the Tele a "pure workman's tool," adding, "Its design was all function." Steve Cropper, a working man's guitarist if ever there was one, would agree. As he told me in 1983, "I think as far as studio work, the Tele over any guitar has a better balance and feel for sitting down and playing. With a Telecaster, you know, you can just sit down, sit back, relax, eat chicken, and play the session."

But from such humble beginnings, all hell soon broke loose. The next model out of the chute, the Stratocaster in 1954, was sculpted to comfortably fit your body, and *its* body was all swoops and curves. Everything about the electric guitar emphasized its futuristic, space-age image. Think about model names like Broadcaser, Telecaster, and Stratocaster, or Gibson's Explorer and Flying V, and Gretsch's Duo-Jet. In the early '70s, Frederick, Maryland's Micro-Frets company had a model called the Orbiter, which looked like a shark's fin and had its own wireless transmitter. And as far back as 1954 brothers Russ and Claude Deaver formed the Stratosphere guitar company in Springfield, Missouri. Not only was its name out of this world, so was its double-neck Stratosphere Twin. Possibly the first double-neck to feature six- and twelve-string necks, its four oddly skewed single-coil pickups sat beneath covers that looked like miniature '49 Mercury grilles.

By 1958, when Fender introduced the Jazzmaster, with its offset waist, and Gibson launched the lightning-bolt Explorer and rocket-shaped Flying V, what should have been obvious to luthiers all along was finally being exercised. A solidbody electric's construction affected its sound, but the body *shape*, per se, had

GUITORGAN BROCHURE
With the promise that your guitar could sound like an accordion, MusiConics of Waco, Texas, offered its Guitorgan.

1954 FENDER ESQUIRE
Opposite page: Detractors called Leo Fender's first solid-body electric Esquire a "canoe paddle." The joke was on them, however. From the first prototype in 1949, the Esquire became the Broadcaster, then the Telecaster, one of the most famed guitars of all time and still in full-bore production today. This black-guard butterscotch Esquire featured just a bridge pickup and minimal tone control—you just plugged in and played, but oh, what a sound! Owner: Strings West. (Photograph © *Vintage Guitar*)

the Duchess

CUSTOM COOL
The Duchess shows off the latest in curvaceous guitar ware—a custom built by Gretsch. The Duchess played her axe with her brother, the king of custom guitars, Bo Diddley.

GRUGGETT
Opposite page: Luthier Bill Gruggett's guitars were a fascinating blend of the weird with the bizarre. A former Mosrite employee, he fused Mosrite features with Hofner's violin shape and created a unique guitar. Just 300-odd examples were built. (Photograph © Teisco Del Rey)

no effect whatsoever. (As if to prove this point, Green Bay, Wisconsin's La Baye company made a guitar called a 2x4, which, as the name implied, was simply a plank. Only forty-five were ever made.) So other than tradition, there was no reason that subsequent models needed to resemble a guitar's shape at all.

In addition to shapes, companies went wild with paint jobs that would be out of the question on acoustic guitars. And Fender gave their colors special names, like Surf Green, Olympic White (as opposed to what—"White"?), and the irresistable Sonic Blue.

So what do you add once you've got a radical shape and a hotrod paint job? Switches, knobs, chrome, and more switches. As Japanese and European companies got into the act, this confluence of over-the-top body shapes, vibrant colors, and more switches than a recording console reached its zenith in the late '60s, at which point you'd be hard pressed to name a country on the planet that didn't boast at least one electric guitar manufacturer. Goya electrics, for example, made by accordion companies from Sweden and Italy, featured glittery finishes and more buttons than an Osterizer.

In more innocent times, such flashiness succeeded, to a point. England's Vox company, for instance, had catalogs picturing thirty-something models of guitars and basses, along with photographs of the Animals, the Rolling Stones, and Paul Revere & the Raiders playing Voxes. Were these guitars as well-built as Fenders and Gibsons? No way. But Vox provided a new look, so Hilton Valentine of the Animals played a white teardrop Mark VI, as did Rolling Stone Brian Jones. And every week on *Where The Action Is*, the Raiders played their asymmetical, six-sided Phantoms. The company soon added on-board electronics to various models—featuring distortion, treble/bass boost, repeat percussion, and even an E note to tune to and a hand-operated wah-wah.

Vox's Mando-Guitar, a short-necked twelve-string shaped like a painter's palette and tuned an octave above standard, was one of the company's coolest innovations. Contrary to legend, however, George Harrison never owned one and did not use one on "If I Needed Someone" (he played his Rickenbacker twelve-string, capoed at the fifth fret).

Although Vox made its first instruments in England, it soon moved production to Italy, where its instruments were made at the same plant that churned out EKO's even bigger line of guitars (and that's just counting the ones bearing the EKO name). Prior to making guitars, the EKO plant built accordions, and it made use of some of the same materials (sheets of metal-flake and mother-of-toilet-seat plastic, slider switches) for its guitars. Importing them by the tens of thousands and helping design models were the LoDuca Brothers of Milwaukee. The early-'60s Model 700 series, with its melting headstock, looked like something Salvador Dali might have dreamt up. Its body, usually metal-flake or some other eye-catching plastic finish on the front with a pearloid back, featured what the company described as a "triple-cutaway" design, due to the scoop taken out of the body's lower-right bout.

EKO also boasted an entire line of violin-shaped models (a six-string, a twelve-string, a bass, and even a six-string bass), as well as solidbody and hollowbody variations of its Rok model. This take-off on the Flying V (sort of a V with shoulders) was named after an English band whose main success was in Italy, singing songs in Italian, including their "Piangi Con Me," which became a hit in America when the Grass Roots covered it—"Let's Live For Today."

Whereas EKO and other Italian makers such as Cruchianelli applied their accordion construction techniques to guitar building, Germany's Hofner company evolved from making violins, as far back as 1887. So it's no accident that it produced the violin-shaped bass that caught Paul McCartney's eye. Even before getting into the rock market, Hofner had a flair for daring designs. Some of its archtops were radical in appearance (including one with an oval-shaped soundhole *and* f-holes that looked like a pair of seals), but adhered to high standards of workmanship. Subsequent models (some shaped like a cross) featured on-board speakers, and select Strat copies (actually ones with finish imperfections) were covered with embossed maroon and gold naugehyde and dubbed the Galaxy. Variations on this model featured what Hofner called

EKO COOL
EKO's Model 700 had it all—whammy bar, accordion-chic pearloid finish, four pickups, three cutaways, and more dials and switches than you could count.

ITALIAN CHIC
Opposite page: A German Elvis munches lunch while leaning on his Italian axe.

its "organ effect," which was nothing more than a spring-loaded volume knob with a little pinky hook, to achieve volume swells. (Some Framuses, like the Strato Deluxe, had the same feature.)

If you were an American kid who got bitten by the guitar bug thanks to McCartney and his mates, chances are your parents didn't run out and buy you a Hofner or Gretsch or Rickenbacker or Gibson or Fender. Your first electric was more likely something like a Silvertone bought at Sears—and if you're lucky, you hung onto it. The Silvertone moniker was applied to guitars produced by various companies, but by far the coolest to wear the name were those built in Neptune, New Jersey, by Nathan Daniel's Danelectro company. Daniel was an electronics buff who, like Leo Fender, didn't play guitar. But that didn't hinder his ability to make an affordable instrument with some surprisingly innovative features that major companies didn't offer (his totally shielded electronics, his neck-tilt adjustment). The tops and backs of his guitars were made of Masonite (the type of material used for pegboards in tool sheds), with a inner semi-hollow frame of wood. The pickup covers were lipstick casings bought from a cosmetics supplier, and the nuts were stamped out of aluminum and screwed on. Plug that baby into the amp that was housed in its case, and you were ready to go. (The amp-in-case models came in two models: a short-scale, one-pickup design; and a full-scale, two-pickup model whose amp/case had the added feature of tremolo.)

Dan-O's Guitarlin was a lyre-shaped six-string with ultra-deep cutaways to provide full access to its thirty-one frets—giving it the combined range of a guitar and a mandolin. It wasn't as popular as the bass version of the body shape, and the Danelectro six-string bass was a staple of studio players, using it to double the upright bass with what they called "tick-tack bass." One of New York's top studio guitarists, Vinnie Bell, designed several models for the company, including the Bellzouki electric twelve-string (its name and body shape a takeoff on the Greek *bouzouki*). And after George Harrison played the Indian sitar on 1965's "Norwegian Wood," Bell came up with a way to approximate the sound on an electric guitar. MCA bought the company from Daniel in late 1967, and

TEISCO DEL REY BROCHURE
You get the chicks with a Teisco Del Rey.

started using its Coral trade name for a new line of guitars. The Coral Electric Sitar was a semi-hollow six-string guitar with thirteen sympathetic strings above the guitar strings (although they don't really resonate much). What gave the guitar its droning quality was its "Sitarmatic" bridge, designed specifically to buzz. Like the six-string bass, Coral's Electric Sitar was one of the weapons in the arsenals of many studio players. You can hear Motown session guitarist Eddie Willis playing one at the beginning of Stevie Wonder's "Signed, Sealed and Delivered," and Bell himself played his invention on numerous sessions. A more stripped-down model without sympathetic strings was issued under the Danelectro name, with a solid gourd-shaped body and matching headstock.

Rivaling the EKO company for the number of different brand names that came out of its factory and surpassing it in the number of guitars it exported to the States was Teisco of Japan. Whereas the LoDucas

estimated that they were importing 10,000 EKOs annually in the early '60s, Barry Hornstein says his company was importing 100,000 Teiscos per year at its peak in the late '60s. Hornstein literally put the Del Rey in Teisco/Del Rey, since his company, WMI, already had "Del Rey" as one of its brand names. No one knows for sure, but Jack Westheimer, who imported Kingston guitars from Japan as far back as 1958, recalls that "Teisco" was an anagram for the Tokyo Electric Instrument and Sound Company or something along those lines.

Hornstein's expertise was in mass marketing, and he says flat out, "We knew we were dealing with kids, and our approach to the market was that kids were buying guitars as an item of apparel." Between Hornstein's know-how and the craftsmanship of the Japanese builders, the company went from something as crude as the short-scale mid-'50s J-5 (which had a nameplate on the back of the headstock that read "Teisco Electric *Guiter*") to models as wild as the stereo Spectrum 5, with its split pickups, multi-colored switches, and wiring too complex to explain here. In between, it made some surprisingly good guitars—like the ET-320, with three square-polepiece pickups, metal pickguard, rocker switches, and 4-and-2 headstock. Some came with a "handle" (or hole) through the body's lower-left bout (a couple of decades before Steve Vai's "monkey grip" Ibanez design), some didn't, and the basses were even better. Another common model is the tulip-shaped 460 and variations thereof. The book *60s Bizarre Guitars* (published by Rittor Music of Tokyo) includes an interview/pictorial on David Lindley and his penchant for Teiscos, and the cover of *Howlin' Wolf—The Chess Box* shows the blues singer holding a Teisco with a built-in speaker. So there you go.

It's a coin toss as to which company made more outlandish designs—America's National/Supro/Valco or Italy's Wandre/Davoli/Avanti/Krundaal/Avalon/Framez/Noble. But what's surprising is that neither made much of a dent into the rock'n'roll market its oddball shapes were no doubt aimed at. The National et. al. electrics were an outgrowth of the Dopyera brothers' companies that invented the National steel resophonic guitar and Dobro. They also made electric Hawaiian-style lap steels, like the National New Yorker, whose art deco design was inspired by the Empire State Building. But when the company began experimenting with "Res-o-glas," its name for the polyester resin and fiberglas it used to mold its bodies, the results were (and still are) mind-boggling. Its name *was* National, after all, so the company decided to make a guitar shaped like a map of the United States—the Glenwood. With its lower cutaway horn dropping off like Florida, its upper cutaway horn extended through New England all the way to Nova Scotia.

A less expensive model licensed to Montgomery Ward stores under the Airline name looked like it was designed with a meat cleaver by a Benihana chef. Because it was favored by Chicago blues slide-winder J. B. Hutto (as well as Jimmy Reed and others), it's sometimes referred to as the "J. B. Hutto Model." Like the Glenwood, it featured a Gumby-shaped headstock.

In *Don't Look Back*, the documentary of Bob Dylan's 1965 tour of England, Dylan walks down a London street and looks in a music store window and starts convulsing with laughter at the sight of some bizarre, cartoon-like electric guitars. These were the creations of Wandre Pelotti (or possibly Pioli), who began making guitars in 1956 or '57. Wild shapes weren't Wandre's only innovation; his necks were aluminum, and essentially a through-body design. On the models I've seen, the plastic body is scooped out, to avoid contact with the pickups, which are attached to the pickguard. The pickups and pickguard, which in the case of the Rock Oval extends further than the ridiculously extreme cutway, are suspended above the odd-shaped body. On models bearing the Noble name, the input jack, push-button pickup selectors, and volume and tone controls are housed in a sort of module that fits into the lower-right bout. You may have seen Buddy Miller, Emmylou Harris' bandleader, playing one of these beauts.

The Krundaal Bikini (also marketed as the Avanti I) featured a detachable, Frisbee-like speaker—or "transistorized electric strolling guitar-amp combo," as the company called it. There was also a model called the Teen Ager, and the Cobra featured Wandre's

DANELECTRO DOUBLE TROUBLE
Danelectro founder Nathan Daniel built inexpensive guitars from cheap-o componentry for sale at rock-bottom prices. Yet these budget guitars have a sound all their own and today command high bucks. These double-necked Dano 6x4 and 6x6 guitars lean against a Danelectro amp. Owner: Freddie Hoover/Hillbilly Guitars. (Photograph © *Vintage Guitar*)

"reverse bridge"—whereby a sort of horseshoe affair went *over* the strings, with the strings threading through individual metal sleeves that acted as bridges.

Back home, somebody must have spiked the water supply in Southern California, because an inordinate amount of strangeness was coming from a seventy-mile radius, centered around San Fernando. In the mid '50s, Mosrite founder Semie Moseley made double-necks for guitar greats Joe Maphis and Larry Collins, combining a standard six-string neck with a shorter neck tuned an octave higher. Later acquiring the Dobro company, he came up with a hybrid electric that was shaped like an ES-335 with two pickups *and* a big pie-plate resonator.

In Arvin, just south of Bakersfield, ex-Mosrite employee Joe Hall launched his own Hallmark company with the think hollow-body Swept Wing, which looked somewhat like a Flying V gliding in the opposite direction. Unfortunately, the only thing this electric shovel was suited for was digging its own grave, and the company vanished almost as quickly as it had appeared.

Another enterprising Mosrite refugee, Bill Gruggett, struck out on his own—which is unfortunately what his line of guitars did as well. He made approximately 300 Gruggetts that bred Mosrite features with Hofner's violin shape, and came out looking like Bullwinkle Moose. (He stayed in the repair and custom-order business, and years later resurrected the Gruggett body style.)

Further south, in Santa Ana, Rickenbacker was enjoying the success of its 330-12 electric twelve-

DANELECTRO BROCHURE
"Shouldn't you be a sitarnick?" asked this 1968 Dano brochure.

string, thanks to its association with George Harrison and a guitarist who ran out and got one as soon as he saw *A Hard Day's Night*, Roger McGuinn of the Byrds. The company offered a less-successful version that could convert from twelve- to six-string by means of a string-grabbing comb. In the early '70s Rick made the 331 six-string, featuring colored lights housed in the transluscent body, which pulsated according to the notes played.

Having been sold to CBS in 1965, Fender proved the adage "what's old is new again" by altering leftover bodies from its slower-selling models and renaming the "new" variations—which ultimately proved even less popular than the originals. Take a scoop out of the Mustang, and it became the Musiclander (also known as the Swinger); shave a little off the body of Fender's electric twelve-string, convert it to a six-string model, and you had the Custom (originally dubbed the Maverick). Fender product manager Babe Simoni came up with those designs as well as Mustangs with racing stripes and pink paisley Teles (actually stickum wallpaper underneath the lacquer). A hollow-body electric called the Coronado featured multi-colored wood—the result of a seven-year process in which dye was injected into trees in Germany!

In San Fernando, Pat Murphy manufactured guitars under the Murph name. The Continental IV was Les Paul-shaped, while the Squire looked more like a Jazzmaster, but it was his "heart-shaped" models that were most striking—a sleeker, more graceful, dynamic-looking arrow shape than the Swept-Wing. Along with a three-quarter-scale six-string, there was a twelve-string model with a foot-long, laminated, pointed headstock.

Whenever I play my Guitorgan live, it never fails to illicit a lot of head-scratching and questions like, "How'd you get your guitar to sound so much like an organ?" To which, I explain, "It *is* an organ, with a built-on guitar" (to quote Waco, Texas inventor Bob Murrell's MusiConics fliers). Murrell, a guitarist with country star Hank Thompson, would literally take organ circuitry (from Baldwin models) and transplant it into the bodies of guitars, then run wires up the truss rod channel to each fret—which was cut into six

BACK AT MELODY RANCH
WITH THE MELOBAR

Walt Smith invented the Melobar, essentially a strap-on lap steel, in the late '60s. Its biggest innovation was its slanted fretboard, allowing one to play steel guitar standing up. Over time, other innovations were added, such as the "sure-grip" Smith Slide Bar, notched rubber "fret guide," pliable mother-of-La-Z-Boy cushion bodies, and the infamous Ms. Pac-Man fingerboard, with tunings and chords spelled out.

The company's early fliers boasted endorsements from such unlikely "instrumentalists" as Pat Boone and Sheb Wooley, of "Purple People Eater" fame. Later confirmed Melobar sightings involved Poco's Rusty Young, David Lindley, Ron Wood, and Cindy Cashdollar. The former Asleep At The

Wheel steel and Dobro specialist, who's played on albums by Bob Dylan, Leon Redbone and others. The red '60s model's body was made by Mosrite, and the wooden "V" features a little kickstand so you can play the stand-up steel sitting down, if you insist. Smith had patents on all sorts of designs and features; unzip the back of Explorer-shaped model's naugehyde cover, and there's a patent number hand-written in Magic Marker on the foam!

After his father's death, Ted Smith took over the company and forged even more innovations until retiring at the end of 2002.

segments, for each string. Nearly ten years before the first guitar synths, he'd already solved the pitch-to-voltage problems they'd encounter by having an instrument that was touch-sensitive (like the keyboard it was subbing for). As long as string was touching fret, the note would sustain. And instead of approximating the sound of an organ, it *delivered* the sound of an organ—especially when played through a Leslie speaker. I did this and got the ultimate compliment when it faked out an engineer who was mixing one of my CDs. As he soloed different tracks, he asked, "Who's playing the Hammond?"

Unfortunately, other than various pointy heavy metal variations, there haven't been many truly unique designs in recent years. Englishman Jim Burns'

airplane-shaped Flyte—introduced in 1974 and originally dubbed the Conchorde after the supersonic Concorde aircraft—was one of the last to flamboyantly depict its era. But it's encouraging, if infrequent, to see innovators like country picker Junior Brown come along with something out of left field like the Guit-Steel. Junior used to play guitar and steel on stage, reaching over his six-string to play the steel breaks on a pedal-less model on legs. One night in a dream, the two instruments melded into one, and he had luthier Michael Stevens turn his dream into reality.

Hopefully the days of dreaming up and dreaming about this space-age instrument called an electric guitar are not over.

The Guitar Mystique

By Ward Meeker

From his "musical" debut lip-synching to The Beatles and pretending to strum his Silvertone guitar, Ward Meeker has gone on to bigger and better things. He is the editor of Vintage Guitar, *a monthly magazine devoted to vintage guitars and other stringed instruments, making him ideally suited to write about the mystique of the guitar.*

MYSTIQUE: *n. An aura of heightened value, interest, or meaning surrounding something, arising from attitudes and beliefs that impute special power or mystery to it.*

If there's a single moment that made the guitar a pop culture icon, it was February 9, 1964. Across the country that night, millions tuned their televisions to *The Ed Sullivan Show* and saw The Beatles play for the first time. Girls swooned. Parents reeled. And boys watched in awe as the power of pop music—and the electric guitar—became glaringly obvious. Sure, there were other famous moments that made the guitar what it is today—Chuck Berry doing the duck walk, Jimi Hendrix playing "The Star Bangled Banner" at Woodstock. But it was The Beatles that first astounded and shocked and won over the world to the guitar.

1950 GIBSON ES-5

At the dawn of the 1950s, the ES-5 was the king of Gibson's electric line. Packing three single-coils onto a laminated-top version of the L-5, the ES-5 was as good as it got. B. B. King rightfully used the king of guitars, as did Aaron "T-Bone" Walker. This ES-5 leans against a 1958 Fender narrow-panel tweed 1x15 Pro. Owner: Mark Baier/Victoria Amps. (Photograph © *Vintage Guitar*)

Twelve years after The Beatles played *The Ed Sullivan Show*, I played Lewis & Clark Elementary in Mandan, North Dakota. On a spring day in 1976, three friends and I took the stage with acoustic guitars scrounged from our homes and performed—that is, lip-synched—"Revolution." Girls swooned (on cue from our music teacher). Parents chuckled. And the peachfuzz on my forearms stood straight up.

Having never really seen The Beatles, I didn't know about *The Ed Sullivan Show* or the Shea Stadium concert. But at that moment, it occurred to me that there was something quite alluring about standing in front of a gathering of people with a guitar strapped over your shoulder (and I'd be willing to bet I was the first to get that fuzzy tone out of an unamplified Silvertone archtop!).

Not long after, I became part of another guitar-fueled pop music phenomenon, this one not so friendly to my teachers and parents. The band was Kiss, and though I got into the music they played, they were all about image. Looking at Kiss was every bit as important as hearing Kiss. My dad even bought an issue of *Playboy* at my request because it contained an interview with the band *and* a double-truck live picture of the band playing live in Japan.

In 1979, I had a paper route that afforded me the luxury of becoming a member of a "record club." The concept was relatively new, and beyond its high prices and lack of current releases, it "offered" the convenient service of automatically sending albums unless you instructed otherwise.

Well, one month I didn't get around to returning the card. And sure as hell, a few weeks later, a record arrived. I cracked the package open to find Van Halen's second album, aptly titled *Van Halen II*. Not knowing a thing about the group, I took a few seconds to scan it. Front cover: band's logo in red and silver on a blue background. Back cover: one photo of each of the band members.

What the . . . ? Where was the cool album art like on my Kiss records? Where were the compelling live photos like on my CCR *Chronicle* album?

For several days, I didn't look at *Van Halen II* again while I pondered whether to take the no-going-back step of removing the plastic wrap. But one night, after tiring of my Styx *The Grand Illusion* and the Steve Miller Band's *Greatest Hits*, I did the unmentionable: I removed the wrap, figuring that if I didn't like it, I could barter it for something better.

Cue the Epiphany.

Coinciding with these events was the period in my life when listening to my dad's stereo at low volume became burdensome. I'd gained an appreciation for volume, and if I needed it loud and private, the big headphones were ready to aid my journey to Tinnitus!

One fateful night after making *Van Halen II* officially unreturnable, I tucked my head between the big Koss 'phones and plopped the record on the turntable.

Those familiar know the album starts with the strange, fade-in, whale-like strains of a bass guitar played solo, starting low and sliding high on the neck. At first, I was startled . . . I yanked the headphones off to gauge my surroundings. No, these bizarre sounds were indeed coming from the turntable, straight into my head.

I pushed them back on in time to hear bassist Michael Anthony do an ascending two-note lick until he reached for more strained highs, accompanied by a phase/flange effect courtesy of the mixing board.

I began to judge. This was not what I'd come to expect from my rock and roll.

Michael continued his game for a few more measures. Then, drums offered up a beat to keep him company. And finally . . . a guitar . . . but subdued . . . like a monster being restrained by the very volume swells it purveyed. When you heard it for the first time, you thought, "Release it, man!"

Then, in the span of just four beats, the three rhythms merged, and for the first time I heard the Van Halen "Brown Sound" guitar tone, panned hard left, meting out punishment to the poor Koss. I didn't know

HEARTS AND HANDS
People from all walks of life are taken by the guitar. Artist Dennis McGregor created this image for the Sisters Folk Festival in Sisters, Oregon. (Artwork © Dennis McGregor)

1960 GIBSON LES PAUL CUSTOM

Gibson introduced its Custom in mid 1954 as a top-of-the-line version of the Les Paul. Due to its sleek neck, the Custom was advertised as "The Fretless Wonder." With gold plating and an imposing array of three humbuckers, it soon became known among players by an even more impressive sobriquet— "The Black Beauty." Owner: Brian Fischer. (Photograph © *Vintage Guitar*)

it at the time, but the very first guitar tone that ever caught my attention is considered by many to be the ultimate example of the form.

Finally, vocalist David Lee Roth joined the fray, and the combo rolled out some of the most grinding, raunchy rock sounds ever recorded—all while doing a tune made famous by Linda Ronstadt!

So I'd discovered Van Halen. And other than what my ears were teaching me, I knew nothing about them, save for the way they looked in the album jacket photos, which told me the singer wore huge bell-bottomed jeans and could do the splits in midair, this Van Halen guy played a black-and-yellow guitar, and the drummer was named Alex and he apparently liked to twirl flaming drum mallets.

But none of that imagery mattered in the glorious days before MTV. In fact, I'd already set the jacket aside so I could simply lay there in the dark, absorbing my destiny.

So, yeah, Edward Van Halen had a lot to do with who and what my "adult personality" is today. And I don't really play guitar. Okay, I do play. But I'm not good. Still, I owe to Eddie the fact that my workaday world as the editor of *Vintage Guitar* magazine revolves around guitars.

Certainly, a thirteen-year-old from North Dakota isn't alone in the world; Eddie Van Halen changed things for most everybody who ever cared about the electric guitar. Some say he saved the guitar's role in rock and roll. Some say he's the reason anyone cares about the electric guitar today.

That may be overstating the import of a single player, but there is no way to overstate the effect the guitar, as an instrument, is capable of having on people. It is a remarkably versatile instrument that, even in the hands of just one player, can convey an immense range of emotions and moods.

And if you've ever seen someone who is *really* good at playing the guitar—Segovia, Les Paul, Chet Atkins, Tommy Emmanuel, Eric Clapton, Steve Vai, Edward Van Halen—you have in all likelihood been made aware of the mystique of the instrument and the many hues it can employ to inspire.

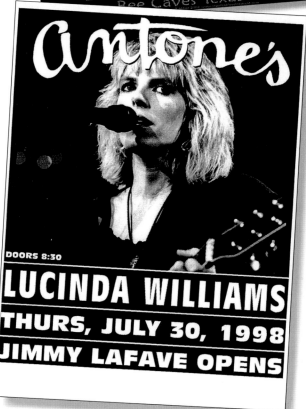

A guitar need not be anything fancy. It's made of simple components that are cut, molded, and fashioned from common woods, metals, and plastics. Sure, it can be fancied up, but the premise is almost banal; a guitar is (to partially quote Webster) "a musical instrument having a large, flat-backed sound box."

And the guitar is one of the easiest instruments to learn to play—albeit one of the most difficult to master. Getting pleasant sounds from it involves no breathing techniques, no embouchure, no positioning of a reed on the lips and tongue, not even a knowledge of musical theory.

There is, however, the awkward process of teaching your fingers to hit the right strings in the right places. You see, the guitar is largely about muscle memory—making the formation of chords and the location of individual notes second nature. In order to be able to reach the pinnacle of what playing a guitar is about—which, one could argue, means being able to

express oneself musically—you must elevate the mechanics of your playing above the thought process.

And it's hard to beat the sensation of hearing the first chord you make—most likely an E, A, D, or G (which, by the way, puts you in reach of thousands of songs in virtually every musical style). And while most instruments—especially brass or woodwinds—can play just one note at a time, a guitar can provide a symphony of sounds with a single pluck or strum. In the hands of experts, one guitar can literally provide the rhythm, melody, and solo elements of a piece of music, simultaneously.

Without so much as hearing a note, neophytes and casual observers can appreciate the beauty of wood that has been pressed and shaped into the form of a guitar. A guitar simply hanging on the wall is an eye-catching thing. Acoustic guitars—especially the finer examples—are made of wood that is pleasing to the eye, as well as elements that command a closer look,

like inlays or soundhole rosette patterns made of pearloid, herringbone bindings, or tortoiseshell pickguards.

The materials alone are beautiful. And though woodworkers often prefer material devoid of "impurities" in their grain pattern, guitar builders typically seek out such characteristics because they give guitars unique personalities in their aesthetics. And these characteristics, bear exotic names like "birdseye," "flame," "book-match," "quilt," and "curl." In the modern world of guitar collecting, the amount of curl on the laminated maple top of a 1950s Gibson Les Paul Standard can drive its price from $40,000 to well beyond $100,000!

And though a guitar can be rudimentarily simple, the craftsmanship of a *good* guitar is a sight to behold. Not only does an acoustic guitar's sides join its back in seamless fashion and necks bow perfectly to support maximum note sustain and tonal accuracy, the best guitars have tops that are tuned to resonate perfectly, with thickness dimensions painstakingly measured to the thousandth of an inch, then tuned by the builder's ear, as he or she taps a finger on it and simply listens. . . .

And what other form of woodwork offers the duality of beauty that is a stringed instrument? They deliver pleasure to two of our senses: A gathering of crafted wood can first astound first via its aural presentation, then upon closer inspection, affect the visual senses similarly.

The "figure" in the wood on an old violin will bring a gleam to the eye of cabinetmaker. The sound of an old violin in the hands of a true talent will touch the soul of any human who has one. Gaze into the maple top of a '59 Les Paul Standard while listening to the "Beano" album, and you just might catch a case of guitar lust severe enough to have you dialing your banker and quitting your job to devote your life to learning chords and scales—and how to put them all together to touch the hearts of man!

Another element that distinguishes guitars from other instruments is the clear demarcation between the centuries-old tradition of the acoustic guitar and the modernity of the decades-old electric. And while some enjoy both, few love them equally. And that's because though both are called "guitars," when you start to pick nits, they bear few resemblances in aesthetics or the sounds they make.

The acoustic guitar is the more pure of the form in terms of its construction and how it is played. Building an acoustic requires greater skill, more tools, and finer woods. Playing it, especially in the realm of classical music, requires formal training and discipline.

The electric guitar came about because of big-band music and its penchant for letting premier players strut their stuff via solo breaks. Players of the saxophone, trumpet, or trombone could utilize the greater dynamic range of their instruments to either blend with the band, or if need be, to stand out during a solo break.

For the guitarist playing an acoustic—even an archtop or resonator guitar developed specifically for increased volume for orchestral guitarists—being heard during solo breaks was a challenge. Then one day,

1959 GIBSON LES PAUL JUNIOR
The Junior was the one-pickup version of the two-pickup Les Paul and three-humbucker Custom. But while it was a less-inexpensive student model, it still boasted tone that won it a place in many guitarists' hearts. Run through a small amp—such as this 1964 Fender Champ—and dialed up to 10, the Junior had a rough-hewn, distorted sound that made it ideal for blues or rock'n'roll. Owner: Victor Lindenheim. (Photograph © *Vintage Guitar*)

someone (exactly who is a source of debate) discovered that by wrapping a coil of wires around a set of magnets and placing them underneath a guitar's steel strings, an electric signal was created and could be amplified. The electric guitar pickup was born, and things started getting funky.

There has always been debate about who was the first to build, market, or popularize the electric guitar. But there is no debate about the form's impact. Once electrified and amplified, the guitar takes on a very different personality, with new sonic capabilities that go far beyond proper hand techniques and sitting posture.

That's why rock and roll and the electric guitar grew up together. Rock and roll has always been a young person's medium, both in terms of performer and audience. And the electric guitar can sound cool even if the player doesn't have the experience and discipline to play it "right." Rebels can learn to make usable sounds on an electric guitar in a relatively short time. And they can do so without having some stuffy teacher show them how.

That's why in some respects playing the guitar has become a near rite of passage in Western culture. Millions—mostly boys, but a growing number of girls as well—have fondled, rented, bought, built, and learned to play the guitar. Why? Because they saw The Beatles on *The Ed Sullivan Show*. Or they heard Eric Clapton on the "Beano" record. Or they heard Scotty Moore play "Heartbreak Hotel," George Harrison play "She Loves You," The Ventures play "Walk, Don't Run," Dick Dale play "Miserlou," Jimi Hendrix play "Purple Haze," Ritchie Blackmore play "Smoke on the Water," Ted Nugent play "Stranglehold," or Eddie Van Halen play "Eruption." That's why. Because when they listened to the radio or their vinyl records, their ears bypassed the vocals and focused on the guitar. Elvis could sing and all, but if you heard more in the tones made by Moore's hollowbody Gibson, you were headed down the path. . . .

And because the electric guitar was still new in the 1950s, it was looked down upon—much like those rebels who grabbed it, turned it up, and started playing it.

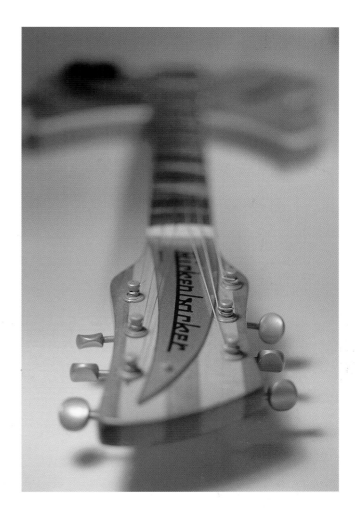

1964 RICKENBACKER 365
Above: Rickenbacker led the way in 1950s and 1960s guitar design with its Space Age styling, swoopy curves, and moderne looks. Owner: Michael Dregni.

GIBSON SUPER 400C
Opposite page: The dream of many a singing cowpoke, Gibson's Super 400 was the Champion of guitars. It featured a solid carved top and regal appointments in all regards. The blonde versions also boasted the choicest woods. It simply didn't get any better than this. (Photograph © *Vintage Guitar*)

In the Beginning There Was Revelation

By Tommy Womack

Since the mid 1980s, Kentucky-born guitarist Tommy Womack has played in clubs across the country with such luminaries as Government Cheese and the Bis-quits. When it comes to his musical style, he has been called "Tom Petty meets the Stooges." When it comes to his prose, he has been named a cross between Hunter S. Thompson and Lester Bangs. Today, the author of the tell-all Cheese Chronicles: The True Story of a Rock 'n' Roll Band You've Never Heard Of, *lives in Nashville, Tennessee. He describes his latest solo effort,* Washington D.C., *as "a greatest-misses hard-rock guitar orgy, recorded in fifty-four minutes—no overdubs, no plastic surgery."*

It was July of 1976. I was thirteen years old when Gene Simmons puked blood and changed my life. It was a beautiful Sunday afternoon, and we were fresh home from church. I was still in my good leisure suit, back in my sister's room watching the somewhat portable Magnavox black-and-white television, lying across her bed on my stomach, digging my Sunday shoes into her pillows and waiting on dinner.

I don't remember what program I was watching. *Hogan's Heroes,* I believe, but I'm not sure. All I remember for certain is the commercial.

Kiss is coming! Friday! July whatever! Typical 30-second ad probably. 60 seconds, maybe. I can still see how it started. Four longhaired geezers from New York in pancake makeup vomiting blood and spewing flame from their mouths, smashing guitars and standing between great gouts of fire that shot out of the ground with fifteen thousand blown-out teenage minds on their feet with spotlights feeling them up. Oh God! Oh God! Yes! Yes!

AWAITING REVELATION
While the clothes might not make the man, an acoustic guitar is a step toward revelation.

I remember it all like it was ten minutes ago, and in vivid color now too, for some odd reason. From then on, nothing mattered but rock and roll. It just looked *so cool!*

It got in my glands. My obsessive streak was torqued. My sister bought *Kiss Alive!* and I pretty much took it away from her. I got their first three albums. Until then, rock and roll had been boring guys who needed shaves, but a bass-player who could breathe fire? That was something else, entirely.

Mom and Dad's reaction could best be summed up as all-consuming and total horror. The Reverend J. C. and Lorene Womack, Cumberland Presbyterians, born under Woodrow Wilson and Warren Harding. Good people who *really did* pick cotton as children. People who worked three jobs with three kids to feed. A father who studied nights to become a real ordained minister. Did they bring the last flesh-of-their-flesh into this world to feed, dress, teach the Lord's Prayer, wipe his bottom, take his temperature and what-all else just to have him fall in with *THIS SHIT? UH, UH!*

The grudge-match began. For the next three years, I daily went toe-to-toe with Mom on the merits of such culturally weighty matters as Ace Frehley's guitar playing, and how it justified papering my whole bedroom in Kiss posters. I had my flared-and-faded, Frampton-loving elder sibs in hopeless squabbles—about whether Peter Criss was a *great drummer*, or how "Calling Dr. Love" was a *great song!*

For the record, Peter Criss was a decent drummer, and "Calling Dr. Love" remains an awesome song.

I spent the next fall down the street, in the front seat of Terry Cates' AMC Gremlin, a truly great car of the '70s. The Gremlin was a Doonesbury eye with wheels on the bottom. We would sit in that thing after school and listen to 8-tracks. We very rarely went anywhere. We would just sit in the car, rock out, and run the battery down.

Terry had *Destroyer, Kiss Alive!,* all the Aerosmith, Brownsville Station, Edgar Winter. You name it. Oh, to once again hear those songs on 8-track in an AMC Gremlin tape deck. That exact same sound. The tape noise. The rumble. The way some songs would fade out. Silence. Ka-chunk! The tape would change channel. The song would fade back in. Cheap Trick's "Clock Strikes Ten" did that. So did Zeppelin's "Ramble On", right before the " . . . but Gollum, in huh *EEEvul* wheyhey . . . crept up and slipped away with herher . . . herher . . . *huhhhhyeh!*" Terry ruled. He had a CB we'd jabber on and at least three different porno mags under his front seat.

I had a very staid and moral preacher's family upbringing. We watched a lot of television, went to the grandparents' place in Arkansas once a year, had no drinking or cussing, and ate fried potatoes every night. Dad did double mortgage payments to get the house paid off before he started falling apart, and he timed it pretty well, too. I drew pictures from the moment I could hold a crayon, and because of that everyone thought I was going to be an artist. As soon as I could write with a fair bit of juvenile flourish, though—about the age of twelve—I took that up. Then, everyone thought I was going to be an artist and writer. Those media were way too static for my tastes, however. Nothing jumped around or exploded. Then I saw that Kiss commercial when I was thirteen, and nothing else ever mattered from then on.

1977. Jeans were still flared, but *cuffed*, in some weird fashion pupal stage. Every girl in school had the Dorothy Hamill haircut, the short wedge thing. You'd call a girl by name from behind, she'd turn around and

1960s GIBSON L-5 CES DUO
Gibson seemed reluctant to enter the Electric Age with its flagship carved-top hollow bodies. The acoustic L-5 had long been Gibson's pride, alongside the Super 400; both were used by the top rhythm guitarists in jazz big bands everywhere. It wasn't until 1951 that Gibson offered ES—for "Electric Spanish"—versions of either. These arrived some sixteen years after Gibson's ES-150 made its debut in 1936 and took the jazz world by storm in the hands of an adventurous young guitarist named Charlie Christian playing with Benny Goodman's trendsetting swing band. The sharp Florentine cutaway L-5 CES at left dates from 1962; the rounded Venetian cut L-5 CES is from 1961. Owner: Craig Brody. (Photograph © *Vintage Guitar*)

1950s GIBSON ES-5 TRIO
A bevy of Gibson blonde beauties. The ES-5 was first offered in 1949 with a triplet of single-coils, as on the center guitar in the style favored by T-Bone Walker. Later versions stepped up to humbuckers and a more efficient control switch, earning them the nickname Switchmasters as used by Carl Perkins. Owner: Elliot Robinson/Thoroughbred Music. (Photograph © *Vintage Guitar*)

UKE PLAYER SALT SHAKER

BEAR CREEK HOLLOWNECK ARTISTS/COLLECTOR'S EDITION HAWAIIAN

Opposite page: Bear Creek luthier Bill Hardin started his repair business early after breaking a uke over his sister's head while watching cartoon character El Kabong, the singing alter-ego of Quick Draw McGraw. After Bill grew up, he worked as a luthier at O.M.I. Dobro and Santa Cruz Guitar Company before starting his own business with his wife B. J. in 1995. Located in Hawaii, they build custom Hawaiian steel guitars in the 1920s Weissenborn tradition as well as custom Koa ukuleles. Bill's Hollowneck Artists/Collector's Edition features a koa body with "rope" binding, a design he collaborated on with musician and historian Bob Brozman. (Courtesy Bear Creek Guitars)

be the wrong girl. Steve Martin was the funniest man on the planet. Star Wars, Travolta Fever, Sex Pistols on the evening news, *If ah kaint have yew, ah don'y wawnt nobody bay-beh! If ah kaint have yew, ah, ah, ah! Oh!* The kid in high school who should have been reading books but was doodling band logos in his notebook? That was me.

In May '78, I got my first guitar, a Stella acoustic for seventeen dollars. I didn't know which end was which. I wish now I'd asked someone earlier, but I didn't. I just sat there at home and tried to figure it out all on my own. After a year, all I'd learned was that those sounds they were getting on those records sure as hell couldn't be pulled out of any seventeen-dollar Stella.

So I got an electric guitar, a Kalamazoo SG copy with white enamel and two pickups. She was a beauty. Sixty-five dollars from Don's House of Music. No amp; didn't need one. I found that if I plugged the guitar into the "mic" jack on the back of my stereo, and moved the "mode" switch halfway between "phono" and "8-track," then I got the record in the left speaker and fairly bitchen destructoblast guitar in the right speaker. Okay, I thought, *this* is fun. Now we're getting somewhere.

Day after day I would come home from school and practice, although "practice" might be too constructive a term for what I was mainly doing, cradling the guitar in my hands while I watched television. I watched ungodly amounts of television. While a large percentage of my classmates were doing drugs at a grand '70s pace—turning their brains into cute little Cornish game hens—I was getting cathode-ray burn on my retinas. The effect is that, to this day, I have about a twelve-minute attention span, followed by the need for a brief commercial message of some sort.

The bedroom, the tube, my records. That was life.

By the time I was seventeen, I wanted to be in a band so bad I could taste it. That's all there was to life any more. Bands. You got together with friends, you talked about bands. You debated who was better. You bought the records and talked about the bands. You bought *CREEM* magazine at Robards Drugs and read about the bands. Bands, bands, bands. And all the bands lived and breathed in some world very far from

mine. Big cities with seamy underbellies. Tough street corners where the kids wore safety pins in their noses. Dark bars at four in the morning. I could read about it all, but it was damned hard to attach any reality to it. There was nothing in my world like it. Nothing at all.

Actually, there *were* two bands my senior year. The first was Archive, named after a Rush album. They did a pretty mean Bachman-Turner Overdrive, and Tim Beeny had a boss, foam-padded, blue-glitter Kustom amp. They did "You Really Got Me" and the required boatload of Skynyrd.

Then there was XBJ, Madisonville's power trio, led by Jeff Calhoun, a great guitarist. He caused a riot on Senior Class Day by continuing to play after Mr. Henry turned the lights on and made it abundantly clear that playtime was over. Hey, can't stop "Stairway to Heaven" midway through, pardner. It sorta builds, takes a while. Last I heard, Jeff was in a Christian rock band with some Hebrew-sounding name I can't remember.

I went to high school football games by myself and pretended the lights and the cheering crowd were all there for me, giving me some sense of adulation I felt I wasn't getting anywhere else. I would stand by the marching band and get off on the big noise they put out, when I wasn't staring at this clarinet girl I had a crush on. I loved our band. They sucked about as much as any high school band sucks, but I loved them. I thought the guy banging the bass drum was eighty times cooler than any Neanderthal out on the field could ever be. Go figure.

I learned to live on the dreams in my head, munching on them like a desperate veal through the bars of a cage. I dreamed rock and roll dreams. Big, ridiculous rock and roll dreams.

May 1980. I graduated from high school. That same month, a band from Athens, Georgia named R.E.M. played their first gig, a keg party in an abandoned church. A hog farmer's son in southern Illinois named Jason Ringenberg was getting ready to move to Nashville and play his music. Big, ridiculous rock and roll dreams.

Off to Western Kentucky University for me. WKU. The Hilltoppers. Bowling Green, in the wavy hills of central Kentucky cave country, where I-65

crosses 31-W. A state school in a tobacco town, where everybody went home for the weekend after classes. No band for Tommy yet, nor likely ever. I stayed in my dorm room and played my Kalamazoo SG copy through those poor old Soundesign speakers. I still didn't know the first thing about tuning it, or even what barre chords were, or how to keep an attention span for a whole piece of music. Ken McGhee down the hall offered me a dollar if I could play a whole song all the way through. Couldn't do it. Didn't know any. What was the point of learning a whole song if I didn't know any other musicians to learn whole songs with? Didn't meet any. Didn't leave the room.

The music. It had gone from Kiss to Cheap Trick to the Kinks and the Stones and the Sex Pistols, Eddy Arnold and B. B. King. It was more than the bands or the sound any more. It was a fountain. A place to dunk my head and live in a better world. It was Van Halen at Roberts Stadium, John Prine in Diddle Arena, Springsteen in Municipal Auditorium. It was a reason to live. I used to drive around in my '74 Ford Maverick aimlessly, with nowhere to go, all alone with my music. *The River*, Nick Lowe's *Labour of Lust* on a weird Canadian label, The Ramones' *Road To Ruin* on the 8-track. If I turned the stereo all the way up, it sounded like Roberts Stadium.

I'd sit in my dorm room with *The Kinks Are The Village Green Preservation Society*, the single greatest album of all time. Buy it today. It's the only album I've gone through four copies of. Come to the end of a side, flip it over, play that side, flip it over, play the other side again, flip it over, the sun comes up, play the other side, flip it over. I was trying to write a song that sounded like "Just Like Starting Over"—with a similar intro, one strum per bar—the minute John Lennon was shot in New York. Years later, on tour, I'd stand in the very spot where he was gunned down. You're not supposed to be able to do that.

If a seventies kid wants to cling to a special date that unites us all, John Lennon's death is all we have, and we have to share even that with the baby-boomers who have always been lording over us as long as we can remember. We place value on significant dates everyone is supposed to commonly relate to somehow. Where were you when Kennedy was shot? Me, I don't

GEARHEAD

Guitar-playing automaton Ezra was the ultimate gearhead with gears even driving his guitar playing. His trusty dog Unk could be relied on to bark in harmony.

could cavort (and still do) with all the panache of the town drunk: slobbering profane acceptance speeches on live awards shows, casually dumping grand pianos out seventh floor hotel room windows, savagely flogging wide-eyed groupies with motorcycle chains and partially thawed fish . . . and wind up half-deified in the process.

There were no rock stars a century ago (save perhaps Paganini and Oscar Wilde), so who filled the need then? Or was there one? Which came first: The need? The role? The market? The song? All I know is this. To stand on a stage with a roomful of like-minded animals, playing a guitar loud enough to kill something, shouting how you feel things oughta be and if you were in charge you bet some shit would get done, and drums are exploding with people screaming and spotlights feeling everybody up and amps are surging this juice . . . Oh God! It looked damn fun. And wouldn't it be fun if you got to do it too?

But you get over that feeling, right? One year, you're twenty, still going to shows and playing air guitar with Angus or Carlos or B. B. Next year, you're some sober-sided tie-rack with legs, buying *Time-Life* compilation CDs market-tested to reach your soul and bring back all those wonderful memories, as if by the time you're twenty-one, all you're supposed to have is memories, and the rest of your life is folderol. The slowest-moving movie-credits ever. The rest of your life, baby. What would you like to do with THE REST OF YOUR LIFE?? Insurance, babies, payments, sour love affairs, fear of death, graduate school, premature baldness—what is it you're going to do with THE REST OF YOUR LIFE???

1984. How did I get here? Still in Bowling Green. I was 21 years old, still playing my guitar on the corner of my bed. No band yet, and I was no less obsessed with it than I'd been all those years before.

It was this monstrous unfulfilled thing in me, this monkey on my back I didn't tell people about. They wouldn't understand. For some reason, life was going to be a mid-tempo waste of time until I'd found me a band to play in. Somehow, that was going to solve everything to me. I just figured that if I was in a band, then that would wipe away every adolescent hang-up and grudge I'd ever nursed. All those pangs of

know. I guess I was fouling my diaper. For that matter, the only time I remember seeing the Beatles on Ed Sullivan was the last time they did the show, when they were stoned and looked like trolls. I'm not a baby-boomer. I barely remember Woodstock. I'm too old to be a Generation X-er. I hated Woodstock '94. All I am is a seventies kid, some poor, dumb sonofabitch who got to *grow up with disco* in Middle America sometime after the great peak of everybody and everything.

And if you grew up in the seventies, you wanted to be a rock star. Oh yes, you did too. Don't give me that. You might not have entertained the fantasy for too long, but it *did* occur to you, at least once or twice, and it was because no one else touched rock stars. Politicians were crooks. Television was lame. Sports figures lacked sass in comparison. Rock stars were the pasty, skinny, stupid and surly sponge idols for every licentious, decadent notion we could come up with. It's a tribute to the power of the music itself, that rock stars

inadequacy would just splinter and sparkle away in the wake of some phoenix-like glittering New Day. If I was in a band . . .

Back and forth I walked to class, wrapping up a broadcasting degree I'd wound up getting without realizing it. Sometimes a broadcasting major is just a theater major with a button-down, a conservative means of letting loose some yearning to perform. It got more ridiculous every day I sat with my guitar on the edge of my bed in a shitty apartment on the corner of 12th and Park. I still didn't know how to tune the damn thing. And singing, well, singing wasn't even worth thinking about.

And so I waltzed in silly exchange. On one hand, I wanted my band! It was out there somewhere, and it was *mine to grab*. On the other hand, I'd somehow become this preppy, myopic dweeb with neither the personality, the musical acumen, nor the cool-school credentials to find *any* band, much less *my* band.

January, 1985. Somehow, I'd graduated. I didn't mean to; it just happened. The check cleared, so they shit me out. Now I was a preppy, myopic dweeb with a BA. An adult. I had a couple of laughable job interviews and nipped all further ones in the bud right away. My diploma went in the sock drawer. I had a Fender Telecaster now, a nice one with a fast neck, and I sat on my bed, playing along with records.

I got a job at Lee's Famous Recipe Fried Chicken. I knew by now that Gene Simmons wasn't the answer, but maybe Paul Westerberg was. And I learned how to fry chicken both regular and extra crispy, and how not to waste flour 'cause everybody's raise is in the bottom of that sack, and I learned how to catch the drippings out of the bottom of the deep-fryer because that's tomorrow's biscuit gravy. I wondered why the hell I was ever born if feeling this way all the time was all there was to living. I wondered where desires come from. I

cursed that Kiss commercial as hard as I cursed the life that came before and made that commercial stand out so attractively. I cursed a society that puts a premium on glitz and makes you think it's somehow worthwhile to be famous and adored from afar. I cursed myself for knowing that fame was bullshit and still wanting to be famous in the face of that knowledge. I cursed WKU for not sending me my diploma after ten phone calls while my on-campus traffic tickets found my mailbox no problem and sometime in January of '85 I helped form a band called Government Cheese.

Was it fun? You bet your ass it was fun. I've come to realize that, in those first couple years of the band, I was the best person I've ever been. I never got any sleep. The band sounded like shit and the whole idea of what we were doing was categorically insane, but every day was a step up and there was a purity and innocence to it all. It was a beautiful thing, and I was fiercely involved. I had enthusiasm and I made it contagious. I was the best person I have ever been in my thirty-two pockmarked cheekwipes of the calendar.

So whenever you drive through Bowling Green (assuming you ever have such an inclination), take the time to wind your way downtown. Be careful—the guy who designed the street layout was apparently drunk at the time—but as you amble around, taking in that lazy bucolic vibe and driving the wrong way up the one-way streets like all visitors do, think of us. There were good times in that town. There were dreams.

I like to think Government Cheese packed a bunch of dreams in a burlap sack and swung it over our heads. While the bag emptied, we kept swinging, and it got lighter and faster, and we spun until we fell down, all dizzy and spent. Those dreams had to go somewhere. They lie where they fall, spread-eagled, pink and healthy forever.

1956 FENDER STRATOCASTER
Leo Fender's Stratocaster was right from day one, and little of true importance was changed over time. This stock sunburst Strat leans against a 1950s Fender TV-front tweed amp. Owner: Anthony Krainik. (Photograph © *Vintage Guitar*)

GRASS-SKIRTED UKIST
Overleaf: With a pineapple uke and imported grass skirt, a lovely lass plays Hawaiian serenades back on the mainland.